DAILY MIRROR, Saturday, September 24, 1904.

THE CRYSTAL PALACE MANAGEMENT REQUEST YOUR CO-OPERATION TO-DAY. (See page 3.)

½d. Daily Mirror

DAILY
MIRROR
DAY
AT THE
Crystal Palace
SATURDAY,
Sept. 24, '04.
ADMIT ONE
Tear out this Coupon and
present it at any of the
Palace Turnstiles.

No. 279. Registered at the G. P. O. as a Newspaper. SATURDAY, SEPTEMBER 24, 1904. One Halfpenny.

LADY CURZON DANGEROUSLY ILL.

"KEIRO."

The palmist, who was brought up at the Clerkenwell Sessions yesterday. He was charged, under the Witchcraft Act of 1735, with pretending to tell fortunes by palmistry.

CUT
OUT
THE
COUPON

A MINIATURE MAN.

This curious little being is believed to belong to a race which existed in pre-historic times. He will appear in London shortly.

LADY VIVIAN.

The charming wife of Lord Vivian, with her pretty little child.—(Photograph by Weston and Sons.)

A deep feeling of sympathy has been aroused throughout the country for the charming wife of the Viceroy of India. She is suffering from acute peritonitis. Sir Thomas Barlow, the King's physician, was hastily summoned from Paris to Walmer Castle, where Lady Curzon is lying in a critical condition.

LORD CURZON.

Lady Curzon's husband. He is almost overcome by grief at the terrible blow which has so suddenly befallen him.

BABY POLARS AT THE ZOO.

One of the two baby Polar bears which have just arrived at Zoological Gardens. They are the pets of the ladies and children, and are as playful as kittens.

PIGMIES AT ST. LOUIS.

One of the queer pigmies looking out of the doorway of his home at the St. Louis Exhibition.

COL. YOUNGHUSBAND.

The leader of the British expedition to Tibet, now on his way back from Lhasa.—(Maull and Fox.)

WORLD 🌐 PRESS

£3

6/18

DAILY MIRROR

ROBERT ALLEN & JOHN FROST

PSL Patrick Stephens, Cambridge

First published 1981

British Library Cataloguing in Publication Data

Allen, Robert
    Daily Mirror.—(World Press)
    1. Daily Mirror
    I. Title II. Frost, John
    III. Series
    072'.1   PN5129.L7D3

    ISBN 0-85059-491-X

Photoset in 10 on 10 pt Baskerville by Manuset Limited,
Baldock, Herts. Printed in Great Britain on 100 gsm
Huntsman Velvet coated cartridge paper, and bound by,
The Garden City Press, Letchworth, for the publishers,
Patrick Stephens Limited, Bar Hill, Cambridge,
CB3 8EL, England.

Contents

Authors' preface

When Marje Proops was told that we intended to compress the entire history of the *Daily Mirror* into a little over 15,000 words she replied 'Gosh!' A very reasonable response in the circumstances. The *Mirror* was founded in 1903 and has battled on ever since, reporting all the great, exciting, terrifying, scandalous, funny and touching events of a century which has not been noted for its tranquillity. But that is not all, for the *Mirror*'s internal history has been as turbulent as anything which has gone on in the outside world. The paper has been presided over by a series of people who look, at first sight, as though they had been invented by a writer of dramatic fiction. There have been financial troubles, palace revolutions, an attempt to suppress the paper and all sorts of mayhem which not only makes the story fascinating but also makes it extremely hard to recount in a few snappy paragraphs. However, we hope that what we have produced will be sufficient to give those unfamiliar with the subject an intriguing insight into the affairs of one of our most exciting national dailies.

We have been helped enormously in our task by a number of extremely busy people who gave up valuable time to offer advice and information. Foremost among these is Mr Tony Miles, the *Mirror*'s Chairman and Editorial Director, who gave the project his blessing and was kind enough to read through the manuscript. We should also like to thank him for permission to reproduce the many pages of the *Mirror* with which we have illustrated our account. Mike Molloy, the Editor, we should also kind enough to read the manuscript. We should also like to thank Harry Cox, the *Mirror*'s librarian, who helped us with advice and information. Mr Philip Zec, the famous cartoonist and former director of the paper, kindly agreed to be interviewed for the book and his reminiscences have helped us to make our account considerably more vivid than it would otherwise have been. Lieutenant-Colonel Peter Bartholomew DSO, the son of Harry Guy

Bartholomew, has been most helpful in providing information about his father's career and has enabled us to gain a deeper insight into Bart's character. Marjorie Proops, Reg Smythe, Ronald Bedford, Peter Reed and Paul Callan, all of whom are well known to *Mirror* readers, have all contributed a great deal to our book and we should like to thank them, too.

Finally, we should like to say a special thank you to Lord 'Manny' Shinwell who kindly read the proofs and provided some additional information.

Readers wishing to investigate the history of the *Mirror* in greater depth are recommended to obtain copies of the books listed below. The works of Hugh Cudlipp are not only particularly useful but also very readable. I should like to take this opportunity to thank Lord Cudlipp for the information contained in his books which has been of the greatest help in compiling this volume.

The Romance of the Daily Mirror, A Daily Mirror publication, 1924. *Publish and be Damned,* Hugh Cudlipp, Dakers, 1953. *Dangerous Estate,* Francis Williams, Longmans, Green & Co Ltd, 1957. *At Your Peril,* Hugh Cudlipp, Weidenfeld & Nicholson, 1962. *The House of Northcliffe,* Paul Ferris, Weidenfeld & Nicholson, 1971. *Walking on the Water,* Hugh Cudlipp, The Bodley Head, 1976.

Vigour and venom

Every now and then a publisher has what he hopes is a brilliant idea. Certainly when Alfred Harmsworth (Lord Northcliffe) launched *The Daily Mirror* on November 2 1903 he thought that he had found the right formula for a popular newspaper. In the very first editorial he spelt out his concept:

'I make no apologies or excuses for the *Daily Mirror*. It is not a hurried or unconsidered adventure. It is the result of a deliberate decision to add to the ranks of daily newspapers one that it is hoped will, by virtue of its individuality, justify its presence in those ranks. It is new, because it represents in journalism a development that is entirely new and modern in the world; it is unlike any other newspaper because it attempts what no other newspaper has ever attempted. It is no mere bulletin of fashion, but a reflection of women's interests, women's thought, women's work. The sane and healthy occupations of domestic life . . .'

Certainly *The Daily Mirror* had been given every advantage since its conception. Trial issues had been produced and a staff of women journalists recruited, among them being the Editor, Mary Howarth, who had been brought in from *The Daily Mail* at a salary of £50 per month. An enormous advertising campaign had been launched and Northcliffe claimed that, 'If there was anyone not aware that the *Mirror* was to be started he must have been deaf, dumb, blind, or all three'.

Everything was set. Now for the only question which really mattered: would the public like it?

Much to the credit of British women, they hated it in droves. The first issue (price 1d) sold 265,217 copies, the second only managed a little over 143,000 and within a few months the circulation was down to a meagre 24,000. The newspaper was losing around £3,000 a week and something drastic had to be done.

However, before looking at the rescue operation let us have a look at the original *Daily Mirror* in some detail. It was a fundamentally silly paper, designed to appeal to those women with enough money and leisure to be able to follow the comings and goings of high society and to ape its manners and fashions. The news, such as it was, had been boiled down to a number of brief paragraphs and, for those who lacked the stamina to read even these snippets, there was a panel entitled 'To-Day's News At a Glance' which further reduced the outside world to a series of single-sentence observations.

'Fifteen persons have been killed and fifty injured in a railway accident near Indianapolis, U.S.A.'

'Miss Joyce Howard, second daughter of Lady Audrey Buller, was married on Saturday to Colonel Arthur Doyle.'

The 15 hapless railway travellers were scarcely better reported in the main body of the paper, receiving only three rather short paragraphs. Miss Howard, however, fared considerably better for, on page 9, her wedding was reported in intimate detail. She was accorded the best part of two columns to herself and there was a most attractive portrait which dominated the entire page. The sub heads tell the story: 'At the Church', 'The Bride's Dress', 'The Princess's Dress', 'Some of the Guests' and, of course, 'Wedding Gifts'.

The rest of that first issue was taken up with items such as 'The Hour-Glass of Fashion', 'Millinery and Latest Dress News from Paris', 'News of Pastimes: Hunting, Golf, etc.', a bit of nonsense in French and the first part of a serial entitled, 'Chance, the Juggler'. For a modern reader the most striking feature of that issue is that it contained very few pictures—and those few were line drawings, not photographs, while the front page, which in later years was to be covered with screaming banner headlines, was entirely taken up with advertisements for dressmakers, a jeweller and a furrier.

It very quickly became clear that the paper was a failure. However, Northcliffe was not the kind of man to accept that sort of news gladly and it was

Lord Northcliffe: 'Women can't write and don't want to read!'

eventually left up to his brother, the financial genius Lord Rothermere, to tell him that his project was doomed. A drastic remedy was required and it started with sending Mary Howarth back to the *Mail* and employing Hamilton Fyfe, aided by Kennedy Jones, as Editor in her place. His first task was to get rid of the women, a sad but necessary duty. They were full of enthusiasm for the paper but just did not have the experience or know-how to produce a successful journal. Added to this they were rapidly acquiring a reputation for quite staggering naivety. Hugh Cudlipp, in his book *Publish and be Damned*, recalls one howler which Kennedy Jones managed to cut before it got into print. A couple who were acting at Drury Lane got married and went on acting as usual, not taking time off for a honeymoon. The paragraph ended, 'The usual performance took place this evening'.

The women were sacked, and Fyfe described it as, 'a horrible experience, like drowning kittens'.

The new *Daily Mirror* was to be quite different from the original; it was to be the first picture paper. The concept was simple enough, but it was made possible only by the efforts of two remarkable men, Arkas Sapt and Hannen Swaffer. Sapt was convinced of the value of picture journalism and, more than that, he had the technical ability to make it a possibility. The problem was to print a large number of pictures, of acceptable quality, at sufficient speed. Sapt, who was employed on a commission basis, managed to produce 24,000

copies per hour and this was enough for the paper to be relaunched on January 25 1904 as *The Daily Illustrated Mirror*. Swaffer was the art editor and he too knew the effect which good photographs would have on the *Mirror*'s sales. On January 28 the price was reduced to one halfpenny and this, coupled with the new look of the paper, boosted circulation to 71,690 copies, and within three weeks it had reached 120,000.

The new paper had little in common with its predecessor; it now specialised in hard news and it ensured that wherever possible it had the photographs to illustrate its stories. The Russo-Japanese war was hotting up and, by the summer of 1904, the Japanese were besieging Port Arthur. The *Mirror* was there to take pictures. At the time the Japanese were our allies and the Russians, then as now, were threatening our interests in the Middle East. The first photographs which the *Mirror* ever printed were of Admiral Tora Ijuin and some Japanese sailors doing gun drill. That war was to be a great training ground for the journalists of the new paper. In order to produce the kind of copy which the newspaper required they had to be prepared to go anywhere and then rush their material home by absolutely any means available. Datelines started to appear which proudly stated 'From our own correspondent' and came from as far away as Russia.

However, not all the stories were as dramatic as the Russian war. From the same country came a report of a theatrical performance in Kiev in which the actor who was playing the villain went on stage drunk. As he advanced on the defenceless heroine a Colonel in the audience decided that he could stand no more. He leapt on to the stage brandishing his sword, grasped the heroine round the waist and advanced menacingly on the villain, who sobered up with remarkable speed. The unfortunate actor tried to defend himself with his stage sword but the Colonel, who had the distinct advantage of a sword made of steel, cut this in half and chased the terrified man from the stage. He then turned to accept the wild applause of the audience and announce that he had saved the Russian uniform from being besmirched by a drunken scoundrel.

These were eventful years, certainly the period up to the First World War was not the quiet, dreamy Edwardian England of the wishful thinkers. There was always war, or the threat of it, somewhere and Britain, still the hub of an enormous empire, was continually having to show the flag. Thus in September 1904 the *Mirror* was able to report the return of Colonel Younghusband from Tibet, where he had been sent to encourage a respectful attitude towards the British Government.

Apparently the porters, native traders and beggars had been sorry to see the British leave since they had provided a useful source of income but, commented the *Mirror* man, 'the better classes and officials looked pleased'. The same issue which reported Younghusband's success was full of other curious items. For example a 'Queer Wee Man' had been found in Lower Burma and brought to London for the general amazement and delight of the populace. He was dubbed the Fairy Prince, probably because nobody could pronounce his real name, Smaun Sing Hpoo. The *Mirror* carried a photograph and a description of this phenomenon: 'Now he is twenty-two years of age, under three feet in height, weighs nine kilogrammes, has a foot four and a half inches long, and a thumb which only measures one inch.

'He is no dwarf, but a miniature man, who smokes, drinks, and flirts with great ardour.'

In addition to all this the paper had reports of highwaymen in Dagenham, a girl housebreaker in Birkenhead, a brigade of women warriors in Russia and the workhouse in Clitheroe had become so popular that tramps were applying for admission at the rate of 400 a week. But with all this going on there was still room for a blast against those who indulged in a strange new fashion: hatlessness. Apparently Leeds had become the centre of this particular vice, and the outraged hat wearers of the rest of Britain could only hope that a cold autumn would bring the 'hatless brigade' to their senses.

If all this was not enough to persuade you to buy a *Mirror* then there was more. For a mere 2/11d you could send in a photograph of yourself and have a water-colour miniature painted from it. The same issue also contained a coupon, your 'passport to pleasure' which entitled you to free entry to a day of unrivalled celebrations at Crystal Palace. There was also a voting slip so that you could take part in judging a beauty competition.

Certainly *The Daily Mirror* (the word 'Illustrated' was soon dropped) was a changed newspaper. In under a year it had gone from being dull, silly and inconsequential to being a lively, informative and amusing paper which people really wanted to read. Special issues were produced which featured beauty contests or information and gossip about the theatre.

In spite of its new image the paper still had problems. But they were now the problems of success not those of failure. The premises at 2, Carmelite Street were no longer adequate and the whole enterprise had to be moved lock, stock and barrel. In January 1905 the paper started up at its new home at 12, Whitefriars Street; but to move a newspaper is no easy business. The last issue in the

The first issue of the new paper. The front page was not exactly eye-catching and the rest of the contents were dull stuff.

old premises was printed on Saturday January 21, and even before printing was finished the move had begun. Not an issue could be lost, so it was imperative that Monday's edition should appear on time. Typically the *Mirror* turned what was an irritating problem into a news story and entitled it 'Daily Mirror's Magic Move':

'In the small hours of Saturday, 300 sturdy men with carts, hoisting machines, screw jacks, ropes, and no end of appliances, besides brawny arms, moved the whole *Daily Mirror* machinery, furniture, telephones, desks, type, papers, photographs, stereo-typing plant—everything, in fact, that goes to the production of a newspaper. The weight of this exceeded 70,000 lb—its cost was something heavy also.'

In 1924, to celebrate its coming of age, the *Mirror* published a book called *The Romance of the Daily Mirror*. It cost 1/- and told some fascinating stories of the early days and the dreadful difficulties under which the paper had been produced. On one

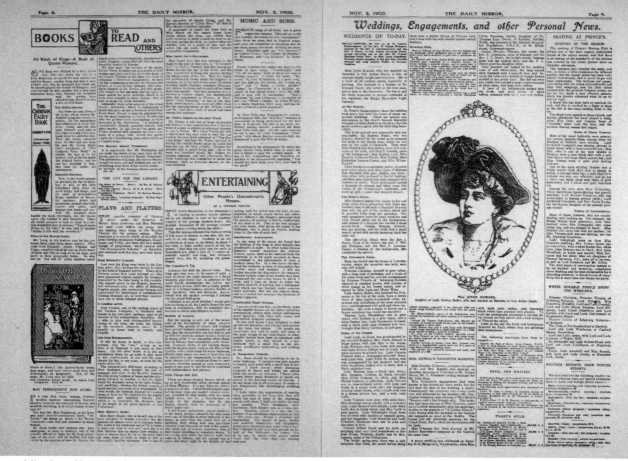

Miss Joyce Howard, whose marriage to Col Arthur Doyle was the main subject of interest in the first issue. Notice that all the illustrations were line-drawings; there were, as yet, no photographs at all.

occasion it was decided to give the newspaper a distinctive look by printing it in blue ink. In those days the printing was done from semi-circular metal plates which, when used, were melted down and used again. However, the blue ink had an unfortunate chemical reaction with the molten metal and, quite unexpectedly, the mixture curdled and produced a nasty brittle mess, full of air bubbles.

The years leading up to the First World War were crowded with incident and the British public was hungry not only for news, but for news in pictures. The front page photograph, which had first appeared in March 1904, had become the paper's most notable feature and remained so for many years. The demand for new, interesting and exciting photographs was such that the public were invited to submit their own efforts, with a fee for any which were accepted.

There was no shortage of news, from great events like the launching of the *Lusitania* (and its sinking some years later), to anarchist bombings, political assassinations, great murder trials and national disasters such as the death of Captain Scott. The

Mirror knew how to be serious, but it also knew the knack of livening the diet with bits of nonsense. Although it was to undergo some pretty radical changes before assuming the style we know today, the mixture of the weighty and the trivial is something which it has always done particularly well. On the weighty side it had already become a campaigning paper. It was discovered that tinned meat, imported from the USA, was so disgusting that even the inmates of workhouses would not eat it. The *Mirror* launched an attack on the import of this rubbish and the paper's cartoonist, Mr Haselden, whose work was usually gentle in its humour, satirised the American meat industry in a particularly vicious lampoon.

There was also drama to be found in the *Mirror*'s pages and some of the news stories read like extracts from Arthur Conan Doyle or Sax Rohmer. For example, in 1906 Sir Halliday Macartney died and his obituary included an account of his career as an employee of the Chinese Dowager Empress Tz'u-hsi, a villains' villain if ever there was one. He had been involved in the kidnapping in London of Dr Sun Yat Sen, who was eventually to become the first

President of the Chinese Republic. The unfortunate doctor was passing the Chinese Legation when he was promptly seized and hustled inside where he was greeted by Macartney who exclaimed, 'Here's China for you' and went on to tell him that instructions for his disposal were awaited from Peking. Luckily for Sun Yat Sen the Foreign Office was not as keen as Sir Halliday on the Empress Dowager and demanded the prisoner's release.

Another drama was the murder, at the Imperial Institute, of Sir Curzon Wyllie, an important Anglo-Indian official. An Indian student named Madan Lal Dhingra shot not only the Colonel, but also a Parsee physician who was standing nearby. The *Mirror* reporter who covered the case was off on the trail of sedition in our midst. A mysterious residence called India House was discovered in Highgate and it was from here that 'the notorious Mr Krishnavarma', a well-known subversive, was supposedly spreading sedition. There was general horror all round and Oxford University, which had previously accepted £1,000 from Krishnavarma to fund a lectureship, returned the money because it, 'was humiliated by its obligation to a man who glorified assassins as martyrs'.

Sometimes even the most serious stories took on the air of a farce. For example, a clergyman was reported to have made a 'very determined attempt at suicide' when he hired a boat at Weymouth, rowed out to sea, took poison, cut his throat and jumped overboard. When he was rescued it was discovered that he also had a length of rope in his pocket with which to throttle himself if all else failed. In spite of these elaborate preparations he did not succeed and the *Mirror* report ended: 'The doctors state that there is hope of recovery'.

One of the most important features of any newspaper must be its leading article; that piece of political or economic criticism which states the editorial opinion of current events. Nowadays, as we shall see later, the *Mirror* is famous for its brash, hard-hitting editorials. But in the early 20th century the leaders took a very different tone. In the first place they were quite frequently not concerned with politics at all. In fact a wide range of topics came up for discussion including Calvin's ideas on predestination and whether or not it was wise to keep old letters (the leader writer came out against both Calvin and letter keepers). Even at the outbreak of the First World War the leading articles

As the Russo-Japanese war got going it provided the Mirror *with an opportunity to start producing some real news photographs. The centre-spread of pictures was called 'The "Daily Mirror" Cinematograph'. This shot, of Japanese soldiers giving first aid to a wounded Russian soldier near Liao-yang, shows the great willingness of the paper to portray our Japanese allies in a good light.*

The Daily Mirror

THE MORNING JOURNAL WITH THE SECOND LARGEST NET SALE.

No. 1,773.   SATURDAY, JULY 3, 1909.   One Halfpenny.

POLITICAL ASSASSINATION IN THE IMPERIAL INSTITUTE: SIR W. CURZON WYLLIE, WHO WAS MURDERED, AND LADY WYLLIE, HIS BEREAVED WIFE.

The murder of Sir Curzon Wyllie by an Indian student in the heart of London shocked people to the core. The fear of a plot by subversives to spread sedition in the capital of the Empire was very real and the Press extracted the maximum mileage out of it.

retained a calm, almost scholarly tone. When George Bernard Shaw stated that, in the first place, Great Britain was as responsible for the war as Germany, and secondly that there were no atrocities which the Germans committed which we would not commit as well, he was rebuked in the tones of a sorrowful headmaster. Obviously Shaw's outburst had been a product of his Irish contrariness. The leader writer always signed himself 'WM'—a signature which was to become famous many years later.

But we are jumping ahead, the war was still five years away and the *Mirror* still had other concerns, some weightier than others. In America there was a scandal over the use of the Third Degree, a polite term for the torture which the American police used in questioning suspects. At home there was another scandal. Entitled 'Broughams for Poplar Paupers' the *Mirror* ran an article discussing allegations made by the Poplar Municipal Alliance, 'a body which is courageously carrying out a campaign against what they deem to be an extravagant expenditure of

public money'. Among many charges of extravagance on the part of those who ran the Poplar Workhouse was one that, 'paupers who had got jobs to go to in the country had been taken from the workhouse to the station in a brougham [a kind of horse-drawn carriage]'. Yet this attack was not characteristic of the paper for, a few years before, it had run a scheme in which 100 unemployed men were paid 3/6d each for a day spent sweeping the streets. The scheme was such a success that eventually over 15,000 men were employed in this way and paid for by public subscriptions.

Although life could be very bleak for the Edwardian poor, for the middle classes it was pleasant enough. And much of the *Mirror*'s content reflected the easy-going lifestyle of the better off. It seems that in 1909 mothers all over the land were faced with an unforseen crisis. Young girls, with that gift for annoying their parents which in more recent times has given birth to rock music and punk, had discovered a new craze—the jigsaw puzzle! 'Should Mothers Encourage Their Daughters to Abandon Themselves to the Fascination of Such Fashionable Games as Jig-Saw, or Should They Forbid Them to Occupy Their Time Over Them?' asked the paper in a headline just a trifle longer than those we are now used to. The short answer was, apparently, that the jig-saw was not a force for evil, 'provided it does not occupy too much time nor prevent its devotees from undertaking and fulfilling the duties of ordinary existence'.

Probably one of the most exciting stories, even for a modern reader, was that of the trial of Dr Crippen in 1910. Murder cases are, of course, still great sellers of newspapers and the more grisly the details, the more papers you sell. But in Crippen's day there was the added element of the death penalty. Although it was only abolished quite recently it is easy to forget the electric atmosphere which resulted when, at any moment, the wrong answer to a question could send a man on the 'eight o'clock walk'. Crippen remained calm throughout his trial, though occasionally he became testy when asked the same questions over again. His cross examination went on and on, but the *Mirror* reported it in blow-by-blow detail and the tension throughout is remarkable. Much of the account reads like a novel, for example:

'Benevolent, wise, acute, the Lord Chief Justice of England, from the bench, himself searchingly examined the prisoner, as he leaned on the front of the witness-box, and the auditors of this remarkable duologue were hushed and thrilled and awed for fifteen minutes, while the deft probing of Crippen's very soul proceeded before their very eyes.'

However, though this was all very exciting in itself, there was an added bonus for the *Mirror* reporter. During a pause in the proceedings in which the jurors were asked to examine some exhibits, Crippen was seen to take out a copy of *The Daily Mirror* and settle down to read it.

Another criminal case which was given the full treatment was the famous 'Siege of Sidney Street'. At the end of 1910 there had been a jewel robbery in Houndsditch, a part of east London, and the police who tried to catch the gang had been gunned down. The search for those of the gang who had escaped was intense and eventually they were tracked down to a house at 100, Sidney Street. Winston Churchill was Home Secretary and took charge of the operation personally. There were massive movements of armed police, not to mention the Scots Guards, and the whole area was sealed off. Naturally the *Mirror* produced a most dramatic series of pictures, but nobody ever got a good look at Peter the Painter who was popularly, but wrongly, supposed to be the ringleader. Near the end of the siege the house caught fire and only the charred bodies of two men were recovered.

The other big picture stories immediately prior to the war were the sinking of the *Titanic* and the death of Captain Scott. Here the *Mirror* excelled itself in picture coverage. There were numerous photographs of the crew and passengers on board the *Titanic*, as well as shots of the inside of the ship and a copy of a telegram to the wife of one of the ship's officers telling her that her husband was among those saved.

Probably the biggest story of that early era was the death of Scott of the Antarctic. In February 1913 there was a memorial number which was almost entirely devoted to the details of Scott and his colleagues. The pictures were given their usual prominence and every aspect of Scott's life was discussed in the greatest detail. This was indeed to be a hero's death. In May of the same year the story was revived because a photograph of Scott's grave had been obtained. Once more there was a very full account of the whole tragedy and the hero worship was revived—even 'Thought for today' was infected by the feeling of pathos and quoted Horace: 'Sweet and seemly is it to lay down one's life for one's country'.

The biggest pictorial scoop which the paper achieved in those pre-war years was the photograph of King Edward VII as he lay dead. On May 21 1910 there was an Edward VII memorial number and the centre spread was taken up with the photograph of the dead king. It later transpired that the court photographer has been persuaded, for a fee, to go to Queen Alexandra and ask her if the picture could be used. By a happy coincidence the *Mirror* was her favourite paper and she said she would give them her permission and nobody else. But in addition to this being a remarkable scoop there was also certain suggestions of things to come, for some people complained that the *Mirror* had shown great bad taste in intruding on private grief in order to get a good story. A charge which had not been levelled at the paper for the last time, by any means.

In 1914 there were two momentous events which preceeded the outbreak of war. In January, Lord Northcliffe sold the paper to his brother Lord Rothermere. The price, significantly, was £100,000, the amount he had lost on the paper in its early days. The effects of this change will be discussed later, but what were the reasons for it? At

The death of Edward VII provided the Mirror *with its first real picture scoop. An intrusion into private grief or a smart piece of journalism? As photography became more important to newspapers this was to be a frequent question.*

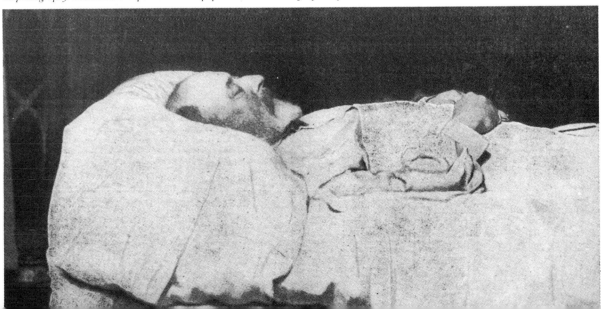

The trial of Dr Crippen and Miss Le Neve was a cause of great public excitement. Eventually Crippen was hanged for the murder of his wife.

the time Northcliffe merely said that he wanted 'to concentrate his energies and limit his activities'. But did this sound like the self-styled Lord Vigour and Venom, Napoleon of Fleet Street? It is, of course, possible that the *Mirror* had become boring to its owner. He had nurtured it from failure to success and seen it achieve a remarkable breakthrough in the field of British journalism. However, it is also possible that the two brothers, who increasingly failed to agree with each other, arranged the transfer of the *Mirror* as a sort of parting of the ways. Whatever the reason it was a decision which was to have almost catastrophic consequences.

In July 1914 the newspaper published a very unusual document. It was a telegram to the Editor from King George and Queen Mary congratulating him on achieving a circulation of 1,000,000 copies per day. This was a new world record and it meant that the *Mirror* would enter the war with a larger audience than any other paper.

The First World War is a story too long to be told here. But it was a conflict which was to affect the *Mirror* in a number of ways. In the first place who could provide the world's best team of photographers? And which paper had the greatest experience in war-time photo-journalism? The *Mirror* decided to make use of its long experience and to provide the newspaper-buying public with the best possible picture coverage of the war. Money prizes were offered for the best war pictures and one lucky amateur won £1,000 for a picture of the sinking of the *Falaba*.

The *Mirror* was not only popular with the troops, it also had sufficient prestige to persuade the authorities to let it publish the first ever photographs of the tanks, a new weapon which was to revolutionise warfare. But *Mirror* photographers were now working, when in the field, in conditions such as they had never faced before. Photography then was not as easy and convenient as it has since become; it required the careful handling of delicate plates. One photographer, working in a small French town, had to improvise a darkroom in a bath. He got in and his colleagues covered him with blankets to keep out the light. Everything went well until he accidentally pushed the old lever-type tap with his foot and the bath began to fill with water. What to do? If he got out the plates would be ruined, but if he stayed in and the plates got wet the result would be the same. At last he finished, just in the nick of time, and the photographs were saved.

Back at home the paper was experiencing considerable difficulties. Many of the men were called up and women had to take over a lot of the clerical jobs. A much more serious problem was that the services were commandeering the paper's photographic equipment. The Royal Flying Corps took lenses for reconnaissance work, essential for the war effort, of course, but very difficult when you are trying to produce a newspaper.

Then there were air-raids. As soon as one was expected the Night Editor would signal to the staff with a green light and everyone would retire to the basement until it was all clear. In 1914 the *Mirror* had averaged 22 pages, but by 1917 it had been reduced to eight. People were encouraged to share their copy and newsagents were prohibited by law from returning unsold copies—to avoid waste—so it was essential to judge very carefully how many papers would be needed.

As our pictures show, the *Mirror* did a superb job in its coverage of the war and it emerged after the Armistice as the first truly mass circulation newspaper this country had ever had. It should have been at the start of an era of unparalleled success, but there were troubles waiting for the paper which no-one had yet even suspected, and the worst of these was to be its owner.

BRAVE BRITISH WOMEN REMAIN AT HANKOW IN ORDER TO TEND THE WOUNDED.

Regardless of any danger to themselves, four British women are remaining at their posts at Hankow in order to render medical and nursing service. Among them are Miss Isabella Wilkinson, M.B., and Miss Booth. Hankow is to be the scene of the approach-ing conflict between the rebels and Government troops. (1) Miss Gooch (A) engaged in educational work, Dr. Wilkinson, who is an Australian (B), and Miss Booth (C). (2) Miss Booth with her adopted son, Chu Tsen.

Above *As China threw off the shackles of its imperial past and became a republic the* Mirror *reported on British nurses in Hankow who refused to leave their posts and flee from the fighting.* **Below** *Home Secretary Winston Churchill heads a group of armed policemen at the Siege of Sydney Street. The* Mirror *devoted an entire issue to these dramatic events.*

Left *The advertisements of this period are interesting and demonstrate the way in which people were preoccupied with their health. There is a touch of irony in the Wincarnis advert for, in the period following the First World War, there was to be an outbreak of Spanish 'flu of such virulence that it killed more people than the war itself.*

Right *Scott's tomb in the Antarctic wastes.*

Below *Captain Scott and his expedition whose death in the Antarctic sent an entire nation into mourning.*

THE DAILY MIRROR, MAY 21, 1913

TRIUMPH BEFORE DEATH: THE FIVE HEROES AT THE SOUTH POLE.

Above left *The sinking of the Titanic was a disaster of such proportions that it shocked the world.*

Above *The Mirror in festive mood shortly before the war. An entire issue was given over to the panto season, the shows and their stars.*

Left *King George and Queen Mary congratulate the Mirror on the world record circulation of 1,000,000 copies a day.*

Above right *As the world was plunged into the worst war in human history the Mirror set out to capture the events in some of the most vivid pictures ever seen.*

Above far right *Mr Haselden, the resident cartoonist, was provoked by the war to abandon his usual gentle satire and join the propaganda struggle against the Hun. This is captioned 'Big and Little Willie and Our Recruits'.*

Right *A Zeppelin crashes to earth near Enfield in 1916. It fell from the sky like a ball of fire and its demise gave cause for some grim satisfaction among the British people.*

Left *Outrage as the* Lusitania *is sunk. 'Thus the Huns have carried out their threat to murder innocent people of whatever nationality', stormed the* Mirror.

Below left *Lord Kitchener was drowned while on his way to Russia in June 1916. Although he was mourned publicly there were many who thought his handling of the war had been less than competent.*

Above right *In Russia there was revolution in the air. In Petrograd these soldiers were to be seen with red flags affixed to their field guns.*

Right *A piece of highly emotive propaganda which contrasted our humane treatment of German prisoners with their allegedly brutal treatment of ours. 'The treatment of British prisoners today equals and in some cases even exceeds in horror anything done in former years.'*

THE RE-BIRTH OF RUSSIA: FIRST PHOTOGRAPHS TO REACH ENGLAND OF THE LIGHTNING REVOLUTION IN PETROGRAD.

Barricade erected in one of the principal streets. It is defended by field-pieces, from one of which the red flag is flying.

The amazing Bart

The Daily Mirror came out of the First World War in a very strong position. It had the highest circulation of any paper in the country, a team of highly-trained and widely experienced journalists, and a well-earned reputation as the leading exponent of photo-journalism. All seemed set for a profitable future. However, there were a couple of major, and quite unforeseen, difficulties.

In the first place there was the proprietor. Harold, Lord Rothermere was a financier, not a journalist. Like his brother he had dreams of political power, and these were backed both by his enormous wealth and by influence gained through his newspapers. But though he tried to use the *Mirror* as a campaign platform, his attempts were a complete flop. His political views seemed to sway this way and that, mainly influenced by his like or dislike of the political personalities of the time. In the period immediately following the great War Rothermere was obsessed with the need for national frugality. 'Squandermania' was the new enemy and it had to be stamped out at all costs. Any government expenditure was to be viewed with the greatest suspicion and anything which smacked of official charity was to be vetoed.

The *Mirror* was one of the means which Rothermere used to spread his message. But it was not a popular message and the *Mirror* was supposed to be a popular paper. Nobody wanted to read this dismal stuff day after day; the country, and much of the world, had just been through the four most gruesome years in the history of mankind, a touch of levity was now called for.

Much has been made of the way in which

Rothermere, whilst doing great things with his financial empire, and coming within an ace of achieving his ambition of being the richest man in the country, ruined the *Mirror* with his political misery. Certainly he bought the paper at a time when it had a circulation just over 1,200,000 and, when he sold the last of his shares 17 years later, that figure had declined to about 987,000.

During the war things had gone well enough. Almost any damn fool can sell papers during a war; even though there are enormous production difficulties, you still have a situation where people

Right *Harold, Lord Rothermere had become the* Mirror*'s proprietor at the beginning of the war. His abilities, however, were more as a financier than a journalist. But he was a very impressive man; in fact the Hungarians, with whom he had no very strong connections, wanted him to become their king!*

The war was over but still those ghastly Huns could not be trusted. The Mirror *reported 'Treacherous in defeat as they were in war, the German crews have scuttled their own dishonoured fleet at Scapa Flow'. This young sailor was, apparently, 'a typical Hun 'scuttler''. Well, really, what is one to do with such people?*

want what you are selling, they desperately need to know what is happening. Under its war-time Editor, Alexander Kenealy, the paper had done well. When he died in 1915 an American, Ed Flynn, had taken over and, until he was replaced in 1920 by Alexander Campbell, things went well enough. But it was in those post-war years of the Campbell era that sales really started to decline.

One reason for the decline was that the *Mirror* had become very good at a task which was slowly to become obsolete. Photo-journalism was to be replaced by the cinema news-reels. Who cared about pages of pictures when they could go to the cinema and actually see the pictures move, and eventually even hear them speak?

But there was even more to it than that. The root cause of the paper's post-war decline was not Rothermere's lack of ability, or the decline of photo-journalism, it was simply that the *Mirror* was *boring*. If we take a look at those post-war issues what do we

see? In the first place you could be forgiven for not realising that the war had ever taken place. The world had been turned upside down and given a damn good shaking, and the *Mirror* carried on as if nothing had happened. Ever heard of the Roaring Twenties? Well the *Mirror* certainly did not. The excitement of those years seems to have passed it by. However, if the paper was somewhat dull for its contemporary readers, it is certainly full of interest for us today. Let's take a look at some of the issues in the immediate post-war period.

In June 1919 Alcock and Brown flew the Atlantic in their Vickers-Vimy-Rolls. This feat was given the full front-page treatment. Rothermere had long been an advocate of air power and this story of a British triumph in the air was sure of a good reception. On page three the two pilots were quoted in detail as to how they had managed their exploit. By the time the reader got to page seven he was being treated to a piece of nonsense called 'How Flying May Reform the World':

'Flying will eventually change the character of the world's thought, and will bring a fresher, cleaner flow of ideas into the brain of man . . . What must he think of those who live next to each other and will not speak together? How mean and petty their quarrels and jealousies and hates must seem!

'The true meaning of human intercourse and friendship will come home to him. He will gain an almost divine aspect of the world. He will realise the slightness of human effort.'

The rest of that issue was pretty dull stuff. 'To-day's Gossip', which had never been the paper's most exciting feature, was apparently making a brave attempt to send its readers to sleep. Even the serial, for long one of the *Mirror*'s most popular features, was not up to much:

'Isobel McKane, a charming high-spirited girl, in love with Noel Godfrey, who loves Isobel but resents her treatment of his brother,

'Denis Godfrey, to whom she had been engaged, but whom she did not love. Denis meets with his death through a flying accident.

'Miss Judith, an acrimonious spinster, who keeps house for Noel. She is jealous of Isobel.'

Pretty gripping stuff, eh?

From the point of view of hard news the era was not without its moments of drama. In 1922 Lord Northcliffe died and the whole of the issue was taken up with reports of the death and elaborate tributes to the man who had founded the paper. On the lighter side, Princess Mary was married in 1922 and had her baby christened just one year later. This was the signal for full page pictures and masses of detail about the ceremonies, personalities present, the dresses of the ladies and the arrangements which had been made for the public to view the proceedings. This issue created an all-time record sale.

Probably the most serious event of the period as far as the nation was concerned was the General Strike of 1926. This affected the whole country and, of course, the newspapers only appeared in a highly abbreviated form. The *Mirror* varied during the strike, sometimes looking like a news sheet produced on an office duplicator, but during better times it actually managed to look like a miniature version of its normal self. Like most papers of the time the *Mirror* hinted darkly that the whole thing was a plot engineered by Moscow and took great delight in reporting on those areas where the men had given up the struggle and gone back to work.

In 1927 there was a total eclipse of the sun, reported to be the last visible in Great Britain before 1999. The next year there were serious floods in London which killed 14 people. In October 1930 the airship R101 crashed, killing among its passengers the Air Minister Lord Thomson. A couple of years later there was a mutiny by 300 Dartmoor prisoners which was only put down when warders opened fire on the inmates, wounding between 60 and 70. The *Mirror* dubbed the whole thing the Dartmoor Porridge Mutiny and hired an aeroplane so that they could get some superb aerial shots of the prison.

During much of this period foreign news had not done as well as before. For example, when a couple of British women missionaries were beheaded by Chinese communists ('bandits' as they were described) their gruesome fate only got a brief mention on the inner pages, though they were described as 'heroines'. A couple of days later rival gangsters finally caught up with Jack Diamond, the infamous American hoodlum, and there was a protracted and bloody disagreement between them. Diamond was mortally wounded. He appeared in the *Mirror* wearing a bowler hat and looking for all the world like a British stock-broker.

When, in 1932, the son of Colonel Lindbergh, the famous flier, was kidnapped there was terrific interest in this country. There were photo spreads of the baby, the home, the police looking for the baby, in fact the whole sad episode was given the full treatment.

Before we go any further with this period it is worth looking at the lighter side of life. What were the things which concerned people most? Well, one of them was a pair of animals, a dog and a penguin called Pip and Squeak. They started to appear in a cartoon strip on the children's page and they soon gained quite a following. Eventually Pip and Squeak were joined by a baby rabbit called Wilfred.

Although Northcliffe was no longer the proprietor of the Mirror, *his death in 1922 was marked by a lavish photo-feature detailing his career and achievements. The facts of the death were highly controversial. Publicly he was said to have suffered from a heart disease but there were others who said that syphilis had been responsible for his erratic behaviour and finally—his death.*

Now Wilf was not a highly articulate rabbit, in fact his lines were limited to 'gug', 'nunc' and the occasional 'pah'. However, his arrival sealed the popularity of the cartoon. Soon the strip had its own fan club, the Wilfredian League of Gugnuncs (WLOG for short) and the pets used to make appearances at popular seaside resorts. For some reason which is a trifle hard to understand, their adventures used to appear in French translation on the same page as the cartoon. People took the pets very seriously and they had quite a large following amongst the adults. In fact in June 1927 the *Mirror* carried an offer for those who wanted their very own Wilfred; probably one of the earliest examples of what the Americans have taught us to call spin-off merchandising.

The beauty competition, which the *Mirror* had virtually invented in its earlier years, was still alive and well. In fact there were still special issues which were given over to nothing else. Of course the whole thing was very decorous and the young ladies were

Beauty competitions were always popular and the Mirror *gave over entire issues to them. This one was unusual, though, because when Miss Mackintosh arrived to collect her prize it was found that she was a cripple since childhood who could only walk with the aid of sticks.*

only displayed in the most modest and becoming poses. In fact, so posed were the photographs that one girl, Miss Mackintosh, somewhat surprised everyone by turning up to collect her prize walking with the aid of sticks. She had been crippled from childhood, a fact which was not apparent and not important in the sort of head-and-shoulders portraits which the *Mirror* favoured. The same issue which reported Miss Mackintosh's triumph carried a pompous piece entitled 'The Beauty of Our British Girls—Why They Excel Other Races in Good Looks':

'Whenever I return to England after a sojourn in some alien land I am struck by two things.

'The first is the peace of the English fields and woods, the second is the beauty of the English girls . . .

'The English girl, even when she is not a great beauty, according to the rules, is so often good-looking, as the phrase goes.

'She is confident, easy, tranquil.

'She does not mince, or crawl, or sidle; she has the same glance for a man or woman, a glance of frankness, intelligence, humour. It falls gently and quietly from those clear eyes of blue, or brown, or grey, and lingers long in the memory. How many a wanderer when he thinks of the homeland thinks just of this!'

Then the old fool burst into poetry, but I'll spare you that.

Naturally the war had brought about great changes in society but, as we have already noted, the *Mirror* was not yet much in favour of change. Neither were its readers. Articles discussed 'Why servants are hard to find' and readers' letters seemed preoccupied with the declining moral standards. One reader asked whether it was not disgusting to find people making love on the trains at eight o'clock in the morning. The *Mirror* had the good sense to comment that anyone who *could* do it on a train deserved a medal. Many readers felt compelled to write in about more or less obscure points of religious doctrine and, indeed, no correspondence column of the period was complete unless there was a religious squabble going on.

There was humour, but it was pretty hard to find. A strip called 'Mutt and Jeff' started to appear and told the adventures of a couple of tramps. Like Pip, Squeak and Wilfred it gained enormous popularity and added its name to the language. The other humour was all weak stuff:

'January Jests—Some Jolly Stories You May Not Have Heard Before.

'And how did Willie get on in the history exam?

'Not at all well,' replied the fond mother, 'but what could you expect? They asked him a lot of questions about things which happened long before the poor boy was born!'

Oh yes, very droll.

However, there was unintentional humour of a grisly kind in the case of a commercial traveller, Mr McKenzie, who ran over an old man. He carried the body along on his bonnet for half a mile and then stopped at a garage. When someone pointed out that there was a corpse on the car McKenzie said: 'Dead man on my car? What's he doing there?' A nice try, but he still got nine months' hard labour.

This period in the *Mirror*'s history is best summed up by an editorial which appeared in 1932 and was entitled 'Split the Atom'.

'The two young Cambridge physicists who (they say) have succeeded in splitting the atom have kindly hastened to reassure us by explaining that their achievement has immense scientific, but no *practical*, importance.

'Good! Because the practical consequences and immediate applications of some of these splitting feats are not always pleasant . . . Let it split, so long as it doesn't explode.'

If the *Mirror* had its head firmly in the sand as far as atom splitting was concerned, it could hardly hope to ignore an explosion which was about to take place in its own premises. The paper which had for so long been a daily dose of platitudes for the genteel was about to undergo a revolution.

If, when you think of revolutionaries your mind turns to Trotsky, Lenin or Che Guevara, then you would be unlikely to include Harry Guy Bartholomew in the same club. Yet, though Bart, as he was known, was no leftist fanatic, he did harbour ideas about running a newspaper which were quite unheard of by anyone else in this country. When he gained editorial control of the *Daily Mirror* in 1934 he turned it, in only a few years, from being a sedate and boring journal into the most exciting paper of its day. And yet Bart was no newcomer to the paper, he had been there almost from the beginning.

He had started his career at 14 as an office boy on the *Illustrated Mail*. He had impressed Alfred Harmsworth, the proprietor, who arranged for the boy to attend classes at the Slade School of Art. Bart showed great promise as a future master of the technical side of newspaper production and it was not long before be became Assistant Art Editor on the *Mirror*. He married a Scottish widow called Bertha Broome, 13 years his senior, and this was the start of Bart's famous Jekyll and Hyde character. For in the office he was known as a holy terror with a vocabulary which, even by Fleet Street standards,

Left *An unusual view of Bart as the intrepid aviator. The picture is taken from his flying licence.* **Right** *A more usual picture of Bart. Lord Shinwell said of him: 'In a long experience of public life I have known many famous newspaper personalities . . . among the Greats I would assess Bart . . . he transformed an ordinary paper into one of the most lively and influential'* (photos courtesy of Lt Col Peter Bartholomew).

The Bartlane receiving apparatus.

was remarkably colourful. Yet at home, in the company of his strongly Presbyterian wife, Bart was a mild-mannered man who never swore and never quarrelled.

We have seen how, during those early years, pictures were of ultimate importance to the *Mirror*. Well, it was Bart who was to a large degree responsible for those pictures. He produced his results partly because he worked longer and harder than anyone else, but also because he was amazingly resourceful when problems occurred. When the Prince of Wales was invested at Caernarvon Castle in July 1911 the photographic plates were thrown from the castle wall into an outstretched blanket and rushed to London by motor cycle. This was the sort of stunt which Bart loved and which ensured that the *Mirror* frequently got the best pictures earlier than its rivals.

During the First World War, he was in a reserved occupation but, when his brother was killed in action in 1916, he got Lord Beaverbrook to arrange a commission for him in the Canadian Army and, in 1917, he was sent out to France to arrange photographic coverage of the British Army sector.

After the war Bart was once more involved with the technical development of the paper. He had been made a director at the very early age of 28 in 1913, and his main strength was the ingenuity with

which he pursued the technical development of the newspaper. It was Bart, together with Captain Macfarlane of the New York *Daily News*, who produced a system of sending photographs by radio. The system was known as Bartlane and it was used to transmit pictures across the Atlantic. The result was rather too black and white, but the important thing was that the *Mirror* was able to carry a picture of Tommy Lipton competing with his yacht *Shamrock* in the Americas Cup of 1921. The system was further developed and was responsible for much of the picture coverage which the paper carried during the late twenties. The Lindbergh pictures, for example, were transmitted by Bartlane.

In 1934 Bart was made Managing Director of the *Daily Mirror* and this was the signal for him to turn the whole paper upside down. Lord Francis-Williams, himself a well-known journalist, described Bart as follows:

'The modern *Daily Mirror* is primarily the creation of one man, a rough, tough, erratic and ruthless genius of popular journalism egocentric to a degree notable even in a profession where egomania is an occupational disease: Mr Harry Guy Bartholomew. Bartholomew, who in repose looks like a Church dignitary and in action like a labour boss on the San Francisco waterfront in the tough days, fought his way up from the bottom, piling up anger, frustration and a cynical contempt for the most accepted shibboleths of good taste on the way.'

One other comment on Bart is worth noting before we look at the revolution he created. The *New Statesman* called him:

'The first Englishman who really understood pictures and strips and realised that no one reads more than a few hundred words on any subject.'

The first signs of Bart's control were that the headings started to get larger and blacker. Then larger and blacker still. Bart went for *impact*, a concept which had not yet been grasped in Fleet Street but was already practised in American journalism, of which Bart had made a careful study. He developed the sledgehammer approach to head-lining and he used shock tactics whenever possible. He could make even the undramatic sound important. Take the front page headline 'Sixpence off income tax—the 'dole' to be restored in full'. Well, naturally everyone was pretty pleased about the sixpence, and if they were unemployed the dole was returning not a moment too soon, but if this headline had appeared in the old *Mirror* it would have passed almost unnoticed. The tabloid revolution changed all that. Bart's influence decreed that not only were the headlines to be big, black and dramatic, but the rest of the text was in a bewildering variety of type styles which, though breaking every rule of traditional typography, made the story *look* exciting. The front page also carried pictures of Mr Chamberlain broadcasting his budget proposals and the scene outside his home in Eaton Square when he was about to leave for the House of Commons. But the pictures were also presented in a new and exciting way, they had ragged edges and looked for all the world as if they had been wrenched from the hands of the darkroom boys and thrust into the newspaper at the last second. But it worked, it looked exciting and at last the *Mirror* seemed worth reading again.

But it was no good merely making the paper *look* better; it had got to be *be* better. The *Mirror* started to campaign. Of course, there had been the odd bit of campaigning in the past (remember the tinned meat scandal?) but now there was real fire in the belly. Road safety was one of the issues and the paper was praised by Oliver Stanley, the Minister of Transport, for its efforts. On the same day it published two photographs; one of the overturned trailer of a steam lorry and the other of a crushed pram which the lorry had hit. The baby was unhurt but three adults were injured. Readers were asked for their views on safety and their answers were published.

Now that trick of asking the readers was to be the very key to the new *Mirror*'s success. What did people want to read about? It used to be the Duchess of This or Lord That graciously attending some social function; but now people wanted to read about *real* people, people like themselves, of course! All papers take a different attitude to their readers: *The Times* adopts a tone which is dignified but distant, *The Daily Telegraph* greets its readers with an almost Confucian politeness; the new *Mirror* decided to slap them on the shoulder and invite them in to the kitchen for a cuppa.

Suddenly the whole paper became more human, more concerned with speaking directly to the people who bought it. The terrible journalese which had plagued the paper for years was dropped in favour of plain, simple, straightforward English, the sort people might use themselves. New writers were recruited; Bart would give anyone he liked the look of a chance; after all, the whole paper was now quite unlike anything anyone had ever seen before, so who was to say which writer would succeed and which fail? His most momentous choice must be Bill Connor, who was to write under the name of Cassandra for many years. Bart asked Connor if he could write a column; he didn't know, all he had ever written before was advertising copy for J. Walter Thompson, Bart told him to go and find out. Cassandra was to be the *Mirror*'s biggest success for many years to come. He gazed out at the world

When the child of aviator Colonel Charles Lindbergh was kidnapped and, later, murdered, it made international headlines. These pictures were cabled across the Atlantic using the Bartlane process invented by Harry Guy Bartholomew.

from behind a pair of specs of unsurpassed ugliness and wrote with vigour and wit about what he saw. After years of sycophantic rubbish it must have been marvellous to read articles by a man who would bite anyone anywhere. That was Cassandra, a grouch certainly, but a grouch who knew what annoyed everybody else as much as it annoyed him and was not afraid to take a crack at anybody. And always, however disgruntled and tetchy Cassandra sounded, he managed to give the impression that his heart was in the right place. But more of Cassandra later. He was by no means the only new writer in Bart's tabloid revolution. Some very unlikely people were taken on during the same period. One of these was a young man called Godfrey Winn. He wrote about his garden in Esher, his mother and his dog, Mr Sponge. He also wrote about the personalities of the day and about almost anything else which happened to take his fancy. His column could contain the latest news on how to cook frogs' legs side by side with a bit of gossip about an actress appearing in a Beverley Nichols' revue. Or he could suddenly grab his readers by the heartstrings:

THE DAILY MIRROR, Wednesday, April 18, 1934.

Daily Mirror

Broadcasting - Page 24

THE DAILY PICTURE — NEWSPAPER WITH THE LARGEST NET SALE

No. 9,482. Registered at the G.P.O. as a Newspaper.   WEDNESDAY, APRIL 18, 1934   One Penny

LONDON EMBASSY ROMANCE—P. 2

SIXPENCE OFF INCOME TAX
The "Dole" To Be Restored in Full

MOTOR TAX REDUCED—HALF SALARY CUTS BACK—BUDGET RELIEFS

SIXPENCE off the income tax !

This is the outstanding feature of the Budget introduced in Parliament last night by Mr. Chamberlain, who declared that the case for remission in income tax was overwhelming, although it was impossible to reduce indirect taxation.

"The relief which would confer the most direct benefit on the country, have the greatest psychological effect and impart the most immediate stimulus to trade and employment. would be a reduction in the standard rate of income tax," he added.

The Chancellor's present-for-a-good-boy comes into force next January. It reduces the rate from 5s. to 4s. 6d. in the £. The lower rate will be payable on assessments for the year ended March 31, 1934, due in January and July, 1935 (cost £20,500,000 this year, £24,000,000 in a full year).

Here are other plums in this " prosperity " Budget:—

THE UNEMPLOYED

Unemployment benefit will be restored in full from July 1. There will be a corresponding alteration in the maximum rates of transitional benefits (cost £4,800,000).

LOWER MOTOR VEHICLES TAX

One big surprise is a 25 per cent. reduction—from £1 to 15s.—in the horse-power tax on motor-vehicles. This will come into operation next January (cost £2,200,000 this year, £4,000,000 in a full year).

HALF SALARY CUTS RESTORED

From July 1 next one-half of all salary cuts will be restored. This affects Cabinet Ministers, members of Parliament, Judges, policemen, teachers, Civil Servants, members of the fighting services, insurance doctors and chemists. (Cost £4,000,000 this year; £5,500,000 in a full year). [Budget views page 3; Mr. Chamberlain's speech page 4.]

The Chancellor of the Exchequer making his broadcast speech in the Cabinet Room at No. 10, Downing-street, last night.

Eyes and cameras turned on the man of the moment when Mr. Neville Chamberlain was about to enter his motor-car to be driven to the Houses of Parliament from his home in Eaton-square yesterday.

'But here is a question which I want to ask you . . And you *can* and you *must* answer it.

'Would you like to sit down to your own Christmas dinner knowing that somewhere in one of the Special Areas some child is thanking you for having done more than lip service to the familiar words: "Peace on earth, good will towards men?"'

A bit sentimental? Soppy even? Well yes, Godfrey Winn came in for his share of mockery from people who thought he was a cissy, and a pretentious one at that. But most people loved him. Within a very short time Winn was just about the most successful journalist in the country. His office was inundated with letters from people who felt that he was really talking to *them*.

There were plenty of other new arrivals during those years. Patience Strong the poetess, Peter Wilson the sports writer (The Man They Can't Gag) and also Hugh Cudlipp, a young man who, like Bart himself, was destined to rise to a position of power in the *Mirror*.

Not everyone liked the new paper. The Chairman John Cowley was by no means pleased with what was going on. He was one of the old school who disapproved of sensation and the *Mirror* was now the most sensational paper in the country. But Bart had control and was determined to drag the paper into a new age of journalism. The real crunch came with the abdication crisis in 1936. The *Mirror* supported the king and had very little time for the establishment clique of church and government which was trying to force the monarch's abdication. Cassandra was only too ready to bite a largish chunk out of the odd bishop and it was this sort of behaviour which finally divorced the *Mirror* from its former readers and gained it an entirely new audience. Strangely enough, the king was not over-enthusiastic about the support he was given, he resented the sensational coverage and the huge photographs and banner headlines.

The new *Mirror* was not all sensation and crisis. There was room for a lot of fun too. Strips started to appear in much larger numbers. Now, Ruggles, Belinda Blue Eyes, The Flutters and Buck Ryan all made regular appearances and were received enthusiastically by the new, young readers. Then there was Jane. Originally she appeared in the 'Diary of a Bright Young Thing' and was popular mainly with the girls. Her adventures were funny

Left *The influence of Bart was clearly visible by 1934. Note the use of many type styles and the 'torn' edges of the photographs. Suddenly the presentation of the news was being made exciting.*

In 1936 George McMahon tried to shoot the king. As this shot shows he was quickly subdued by a number of burly policemen including Special Constable Dick (left) — who says you can't trust a Special like an old time copper.

but quite inoffensive and gave no hint of the stir she was to cause in the years to come. But Jane was to be one of those features for which the *Mirror* became famous. One man who did much to promote the use of strips was Basil Nicholson. He greatly admired the American techniques and—as Features Editor—was a major force in Bart's revolution. Unfortunately he was a strong and eccentric personality in his own right and he came into such conflict with Bart that he had to leave.

As the world edged closer and closer to war, Hitler and his clique were much discussed by all the British Press. There were those who favoured appeasement, those who thought he was not as bad as he was made out to be, even those who thought he was a man of destiny who was going to be a great leader. The *Mirror* is still proud of the fact, which it has, with a typical lack of false modesty, pointed out

many times in subsequent years, that it always
called Hitler a villain, always rejected Nazism and
never failed to point out what was going on in the
rest of Europe. In September 1938 there was a
memorable headline even by *Mirror* standards. In
letters inches high it screamed, 'WAR UNLESS
BRITAIN IS STRONG'. The same issue
contained a report from Cassandra who had just
returned from Czechoslovakia, a country which was
expecting to be invaded at any moment. He was at
his vitriolic best:

'I was told that the authorities were fully aware
that such an onslaught would probably mean
anything from seventy-five thousand to one
hundred thousand dead.

'What to do with the bodies?
'Dig pits and fling them in.
'It would take time, of course, to drag them from
the ruins, but it could be done.
'Shocked, are you?
'Appalled?
'Don't be unreasonable!
'It will only be Adolf Hitler rescuing his tortured
Sudeten Germans from the ruthless ferocity of the
Czechs.
'The Saviour among his people again.
'The Second Coming of Our Leader.'

A year later Britain entered the war and the
Mirror began a new phase in its life. How would
this shocking, mannerless, belligerent new paper
survive?

Above *Jack 'Legs' Diamond, the notorious US gangster, looking
worried. He had reason—some 'business rivals' burst into his hotel
and filled him full of lead.* **Below** *The fire which destroyed Crystal
Palace in December 1936. Firemen were forced back by the heat and
by rivers of molten glass.*

Above *Some important figures from* Mirror *history. On the extreme left (seated on the dinghy smoking a cigar) is the young Harry Guy Bartholomew. Sir Harold Harmsworth, wearing a trilby, is on the right of the bench with the Editor, Kenealy, on his left. Hannen Swaffer is second from the right in the third row wearing a large flat cap and bow tie* (photo courtesy of Lt Col Peter Bartholomew). **Below** *The wedding of Princess Mary and Viscount Lascelles was just the sort of royal news for which the British public has always hungered. The royal couple had a child the following year and the christening was also reported with great enthusiasm. These royal issues achieved record circulation.*

Above left *After the First World War there was time for the great achievements of peace. When Alcock and Brown flew the Atlantic in June 1919 they were greeted as national heroes. The Mirror, under Rothermere, was especially keen on the furtherance of the cause of aviation.* **Above right** *Mlle Lenglen, the legendary French tennis player at Wimbledon in the summer of 1919.* **Below** *'Jane's Journal' was a popular feature with young women. In those early days there was no hint of the furore which Jane was to cause later.* **Bottom** *The strip 'Pip, Squeak and Wilfred' was to become something of a cult in Britain.* **Right** *The crash of the airship R101 has gone down in history as a major air disaster. Forty-six people including Lord Thomson, the Air Minister, were burned alive in this terrible mess of twisted metal.*

JANE'S JOURNAL—The Diary of a Bright Young Thing

PIP, SQUEAK AND WILFRED

Pip is now in possession of Auntie's famous book of magic—which contains a "recipe" for catching an invisible person (or penguin). Let's hope it will work!

The DAILY MIRROR, Monday, October 6, 1930.

GREAT AIRSHIP DISASTER: PAGES OF PICTURES

32 PAGES

Daily Mirror
THE DAILY PICTURE PAPER WITH THE LARGEST NET SALE

No. 8,387 — Registered at the G.P.O. as a Newspaper. — MONDAY, OCTOBER 6, 1930 — One Penny

R101 MEMORIAL NUMBER

THE TRAGIC END OF R101
AIR MINISTER AND AIRSHIP EXPERTS LOST—46 VICTIMS

Looking along the wreckage of R 101, which ran into a storm, crashed and burst into flames soon after 2 o'clock yesterday morning at Allonne, near Beauvais, while on an attempted flight to India. Only seven of the crew and an official of the Royal Airship Works at Cardington were saved. Forty-six of those on board, including Lord Thomson, the Air Minister, Sir Sefton Brancker, and famous pioneers of airship development, perished in the flames which consumed the giant airship. It is thought that the airship struck the side of a hill. The explosion following the crash shook Beauvais, four miles away. See also pages 5, 7, 16, 17, 19, 28 and 32.—("Daily Mirror" photograph.)

Far left *In 1927 there was the last total eclipse until 1999.*

Left *During the General Strike of 1926 the paper appeared as either a duplicated news sheet or as a miniature (7½ in by 10⅛ in) version of the usual paper. Bart produced these issues almost single-handed.*

Above and above right *The Mirror's coverage of the abdication crisis was a major landmark in its history. By taking the side of the King against the Church and the political Establishment the paper alienated many of the middle class readers it had appealed to in the past. But the new mood of honesty and controversy was to turn a stuffy, uninspired journal into a giant of the popular press.*

Right *In the late '30s, with the shades of war hanging heavily over Europe, the start of the reign of King George VI was hailed as a bright spot in an otherwise threatening world.*

WEDNESDAY, SEPTEMBER 14, 1938

Daily Mirror

No. 10850   Registered at the G.P.O. as a Newspaper.   ONE PENNY

LONDON ED.

WAR UNLESS
BRITAIN IS STRONG

6 P.M. CHIEFS OF STAFF MET AT

8 P.M. INNER CABINET MET AT

No. 10

Henlein's Attitude

'Plebiscite Only'

SUDETENS ISSUED AN ULTIMATUM TO THE CZECH GOVERNMENT LAST NIGHT, DEMANDING THE RE-CALL OF THE MARTIAL LAW DECREES WITHIN SIX HOURS—"OR WE SHALL NOT BE RESPONSIBLE FOR THE CONSEQUENCES."

The Czech Government, in permanent session, announced that they would ignore the ultimatum which was due to expire at midnight.

Herr Henlein, the Sudeten leader, after a meeting of his party chiefs announced that only a plebiscite would now satisfy the Sudetens. The original eight-point programme is not now enough.

In Russia a Foreign Office spokesman told the " Daily Mirror ": Russia marches as soon as France fights.

In Paris, where M. Daladier, the Premier, is in hourly touch with his chiefs of staff, it was said: " As soon as German troops cross the Czech frontier France mobilises and fights."

PRAGUE : THE FULL STORY—SEE PAGE THREE.

IF FRANCE FIGHTS, BRITAIN FIGHTS. THAT IS THE OFFICIAL ATTITUDE ON THE SITUATION THAT EMERGES AFTER HITLER'S SPEECH AT NUREMBERG.

It is the issue every man and woman in Britain must face.

In Downing-street last night the most important meetings since the Great War took place.

At six o'clock the Premier talked with the chiefs of the fighting forces. At eight o'clock the Inner Cabinet—the Premier, Lord Halifax, Sir John Simon and Sir Samuel Hoare met.

They were joined by the Service Ministers—Sir Thomas Inskip (Defence), Sir Kingsley Wood (Air), Mr. Hore-Belisha (War) and Mr. Duff Cooper (Navy).

If the situation takes a more serious turn certain measures which have long been considered by the Defence Services will be put into operation.—Full story: See Back Page.

DOWNING-STREET LAST NIGHT—SEE BACK PAGE.

Left *On the brink. Although the war is still not quite here yet the* Mirror *had already thrown its weight into the struggle against Hitler. Note the sledgehammer headlines and the use of bold typography. This was to set a style which would stand the* Mirror *in good stead for many years to come.*

Right *This powerful image illustrated Cassandra's report from Prague. It rammed home the danger of a German invasion.*

Below and below right *For a little while it seemed as if the war might not happen . . . and the fascists seemed affable enough.*

Overleaf *However, war was eventually declared, on a Sunday, and the dailies therefore missed out! On the first day of war the* Mirror *welcomed Churchill into the government; it was a relationship which was soon to turn very sour.*

DAILY MIRROR, Monday, September 4, 1939

Daily Mirror

No. 11,152 ✦ ONE PENNY
Registered at the G.P.O. as a Newspaper.

BRITAIN'S FIRST DAY OF WAR: CHURCHILL IS NEW NAVY CHIEF

BRITAIN AND GERMANY HAVE BEEN AT WAR SINCE ELEVEN O'CLOCK YESTERDAY MORNING. FRANCE AND GERMANY HAVE BEEN AT WAR SINCE YESTERDAY AT 5 P.M.

A British War Cabinet of nine members was set up last night. Mr. Winston Churchill, who was First Lord of the Admiralty when Britain last went to war, returns to that post.

Full list of the War Cabinet is:—

PRIME MINISTER: Mr. Neville Chamberlain.
CHANCELLOR OF THE EXCHEQUER:
    Sir John Simon.
FOREIGN SECRETARY: Viscount Halifax.
DEFENCE MINISTER: Lord Chatfield.
FIRST LORD: Mr. Winston Churchill.

SECRETARY FOR WAR:
    Mr. Leslie Hore-Belisha.
SECRETARY FOR AIR: Sir Kingsley Wood.
LORD PRIVY SEAL: Sir Samuel Hoare.
MINISTER WITHOUT PORTFOLIO:
    Lord Hankey.

There are other Ministerial changes. Mr. Eden becomes Dominions Secretary, Sir Thomas Inskip goes to the House of Lords as Lord Chancellor, Lord Stanhope, ex-First Lord, becomes Lord President of the Council, Sir John Anderson is the Home Secretary and Minister of Home Security—a new title.

None of these is in the Cabinet, which is restricted to the Big Nine. These are the men who will be responsible for carrying on the war.

But Mr. Eden is to have special access to the Cabinet.

The Liberal Party explained last night that although Sir Archibald Sinclair had been offered a ministerial post, the Party had decided at this moment not to enter the Government.

Petrol Will Be Rationed

The first meeting of the new war Cabinet took place last night. Mr. Churchill was the first to leave and the crowd broke into a cheer as he walked out. Mr. Hore-Belisha was driven away by a woman chauffeur in uniform.

The Premier went from Downing-street to Buckingham Palace where he stayed with the King for three-quarters of an hour.

It was announced last night that as from September 16 all petrol will be rationed. In the meantime all car owners are asked not to use their cars more than is vitally necessary.

POLES ATTACK

POLISH troops are fighting on German territory, according to a Warsaw message.

A Polish counter-attack pushed back the Germans and penetrated East Prussia near Deutsch Eylau, it was claimed.

The Polish Embassy in London described a Nazi report that troops had cut the Corridor as "entirely false."

Later (according to the Havas Agency) the Polish Radio announced that Poland had retaken the frontier station of Zbaszyn.

The German News Agency claimed that Nazi troops, operating on the Southern front had taken the town of Radomsko.

Radomsko, north of the industrial region round Kattowitz, is about forty miles from the Polish frontier.

1,500 Raid Casualties

The Poles' latest estimate of casualties in German air raids was issued last night in Warsaw.

It is alleged that 1,500 people were killed or injured in German air bombardment of open towns and villages during Friday and Saturday. A considerable proportion of the victims were women and children.

[The German Government had secured from

Contd. on Bk. Page, Col. I

"BREMEN IS CAPTURED"

—French Report

The £4,000,000 German liner Bremen was reported to have been captured yesterday and taken to a British port.

A report from a high French source stated that the Bremen was captured at 4 p.m., but the area in which the liner was captured was not mentioned.

A French Government radio station broadcast the report which was picked up by the Mutual Broadcasting System of America.—Associated Press and British United Press.

To-day all banks throughout Britain will be closed.

Australia yesterday declared war on Germany. "Where Britain stands, stand the people of the Empire and the British world," said Prime Minister Menzies in a broadcast message last night.

New Zealand has cabled her full support to Britain. There is a rush of recruits in Canada. At Toronto a queue of 2,000 men lined outside the Recruiting Office.

Japan has assured Britain of her neutrality in the present war.

Britain's last two-hour ultimatum to Germany was revealed to the people of Britain in a memorable broadcast from Downing-street by Mr. Chamberlain at 11.15 yesterday morning. By that time

cont'd in Col. 4, Back Page

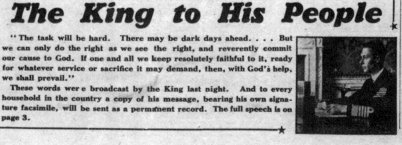

The King to His People

"The task will be hard. There may be dark days ahead. . . . But we can only do the right as we see the right, and reverently commit our cause to God. If one and all we keep resolutely faithful to it, ready for whatever service or sacrifice it may demand, then, with God's help, we shall prevail."

These words were broadcast by the King last night. And to every household in the country a copy of his message, bearing his own signature facsimile, will be sent as a permanent record. The full speech is on page 3.

Rocking the boat

The *Mirror* entered the Second World War in a spirit of 'Up and at 'em' which largely ignored the fact that Britain had very little to get at them with. Even so the paper's enthusiasm for bashing Hitler was considerable and, as a first step towards this objective it was felt that Chamberlain should be given every encouragement to go. As far as the *Mirror* was concerned Churchill was the man of the hour. The headline on September 4 1939 was: 'Britain's First Day of War: Churchill is New Navy Chief'. This partiality to Churchill went back to before the war when both Cecil Harmsworth King (a nephew of Lord Northcliffe and now a director of both the *Mirror* and its companion paper the *Sunday Pictorial*) and Hugh Cudlipp, who had left the *Mirror* to join the *Sunday Pictorial* as its Editor, met Churchill and were impressed by his grasp of the situation. There were not many people, and damn few politicians, who fully realised just how grave things were and how little chance there was of putting them right in time.

The *Mirror* had become firstly and most importantly a young people's paper. It spoke in the language of the ordinary man and its views were expressed simply. Every message was rammed home with bold type, italics, whole sentences in capitals; in fact any device which would make people sit up and take notice. It may not have been very sophisticated, and it was about as subtle as a bullet in the brain, but it was popular.

The earliest targets for the war-time paper were the bureaucrats and bunglers whose red-tape obsessions were holding up the war effort. These people were quickly dubbed The Muddlers and their activities were given front-page prominence in a panel simply headed MUDDLE. Bill Greig launched the column with an appeal to readers to send him instances of muddle which he could print, but he was already able to offer an example of his own. The terrible trials of Mr Acton, a photographic engineer who was unable to get a job

of national importance because the authorities did not recognise such a profession, was paraded as a typical example of a valuable man not being used just because some fool of a clerk had no common sense. This sort of story appealed to the young readers who were impatient with the fussy, pernickety ways of the Civil Service and wanted to get on and *do* something about Hitler.

However, the criticisms did not stop with the bureaucracy; they were to extend to the military command and the politicians. There was no shortage of stupid, trivial and time-wasting regulations dear to the hearts of the army brass hats for the *Mirror* to get its teeth into. These ranged from the trivial ('Why were soldiers on leave not allowed to walk arm in arm with their girlfriends?') to the much more serious. Servicemen were encouraged to write to the paper—which, according to the regulations they were not allowed to do without their commanding officer's approval—and complain about the stupidities of military life. To give the *Mirror* credit, it was not in the business of encouraging whingers and barrack-room lawyers, but was very zealous in looking for examples of inefficiency. Naturally this did not do much for the paper's popularity with the authorities, but it certainly made it lively reading.

However, the real trouble started when the government began to come under attack. Naturally Cassandra was not far from the scene of the crime. A typical column in 1940 looked like this:

'The Government has 'appealed' for the surrender of all shotguns.

'Why are there still plenty for sale in gunsmiths' windows?

'The Government has 'appealed' for people to use less tea.

'Why don't they ration it? The country is about to be besieged.

'The Government has 'appealed' for people to cease joy-riding in cars.

MUDDLE

The Muddlers are holding up Britain's war efforts. They are strangling the wheels of national endeavour in skeins of red tape. This column is dedicated to exposing them. With your help it can be done. Send me the facts and I will print them.

To drive a further nail in the coffin of the Muddlers I shall send the particulars of each case to the Minister concerned. Then we shall see which of them is really anxious to get a move on.—BILL GREIG.

✦ ✦ ✦

MR. F. A. ACTON is a photographic engineer living at Bournemouth. He wants a task of national importance, and wrote to a Reading firm doing Government work to ask if they could use him.

They replied that they had an immediate vacancy for him, but under the Ministry of Labour regulations, he must apply at his local employment exchange and ask them to get in touch with Reading.

Let Mr. Acton tell the story now:

"At the local exchange I was told by a clerk that there was no such trade as photographic engineer in his list of classifications. The nearest he could classify me was as a scientific instrument maker.

"This was Thursday, June 13. I called last Wednesday and was told they would let me know as soon as they heard anything.

"I saw the supervisor again on Monday, and after a long preamble was sent off to a third clerk, who looked up files and said

no reply had been received. Eventually he agreed to send a reminder to Reading.

"I asked him how I was placed if another vacancy arose for a photographic engineer now that I was registered as a scientific instrument maker. He was unable to answer.

"My work entails the use of lathes to fine limits, ability to take micrometer and vernier readings, and I asked if I could do turning work, but was told I must now stick to the trade at which I registered. So I am still waiting to get started in a job which the Ministry of Labour does not officially recognise."

Put in a nutshell—Job ready for man, man ready for job, only the Muddlers keep them apart. Too easy, I suppose, to let a man start work first and go through the formalities afterwards.

I spoke to an official of the Reading firm. "We are desperate for men," he said. "Our work is being held up. We have had this man on our books for a fortnight and still cannot get permission for him to start."

Mr. Acton's letter is going to the Minister of Labour. We shall see if he does anything about it.

EX-PREMIERS ARE HERE

THREE former Premiers of France are now in England. They are:—

M. LEON BLUM, the Socialist leader, who was Prime Minister before M. Daladier, the man of Munich, who was later replaced by M. Reynaud.

M. Herriot, President of the Chamber of Deputies (Speaker of the French Parliament);

M. Paul-Boncour, a moderate Socialist leader.

M. Pierre Cot, a former Air Minister, has been here for some days. Other French leaders of the Left, who favour a "fight on" policy, may be expected, but it is becoming increasingly difficult for such Frenchmen to get out of their country. There is no reliable news of M. Reynaud: there have been reports that he had gone to the U.S.A. Other reports say he is still in France; others that he was placed under open arrest by the Petain faction.

Gold Smuggling Story

M. Blum's secretary has been held by the Spanish police, who say his passport was "irregular."

The German radio, quoting what it described as a Spanish report, alleged last night that three secretaries of M. Reynaud had been arrested at Irun while trying to cross the frontier into Spain.

The radio said they had arrived at Irun in three cars, with a large trunk containing an "immense *Contd. on Back Page, Col. 2*

CHURCHILL SEES THE KING

Mr. Winston Churchill and Sir Ronald Campbell, Ambassador to France, saw the King last night.

Good when you're TIRED

You've had something more than a drink when you've had a GUINNESS

'Why don't they stop it? Have we got inexaustible supplies of petrol?

'The Government has 'appealed' for children to be evacuated.

'Why don't they enforce it?

'The Government has 'appealed' for voluntary savings.

'Why don't they commandeer them? What's the good of fifty pounds in the bank if Hitler wins? . . .

'This Battle for England is being run on a voluntary basis.

'Who'll subscribe to not having his throat cut? No compulsion! No coercion! Heil Magna Carta!'

The Government was not visibly amused by these sort of attacks and Churchill, who had been glad enough to have his views publicised in the *Mirror* in the days when most people did not want to know him, was less amused than most. The *Mirror* had not been slow to notice, and point out to its readers, that many of the old muddlers and appeasers of the pre-Churchill days were still muddling along in the government and that Churchill was not doing much to get rid of them. Cecil King was summoned to see Churchill and explain his conduct in permitting such attacks to be made. King pointed out that the feeling against Chamberlain was strong and that his paper was reporting that feeling accurately. Churchill's view was that he could not afford to trample on the Chamberlain clique because he would only succeed in creating internecine strife which would help the Germans. There was no clear outcome to this quarrel: King felt he had a duty to point out the faults of the administration and Churchill was just as sure that the *Mirror* had a duty to support the government in a most difficult time.

Throughout 1940 the relations between Churchill and the *Mirror* continued to deteriorate. One of the causes of that deterioration was Richard Jennings, the *Mirror*'s leader writer. Jennings had been with the paper since its earliest days, indeed he was 'WM', the man who wrote all those rather arcane articles on obscure subjects. But during the war he changed from being a quiet, intellectual bibliophile and became a fierce defender of our way of life and a scourge to bunglers, muddlers and bureaucrats. Jennings repeatedly stung the government with his political comments, whilst Cassandra poured satirical scorn on a multitude of abuses which were regularly uncovered either by himself or his readers. There was, for example, the 'Gutzkrieg'. Cassandra had discovered that people were eating

Left *By the summer of 1940 relations between the* Mirror *and the government were strained. The 'Muddle' column pointed out defects in the war effort which the politicians would rather have ignored.*

Two editions of the paper for August 16 1940 reported our success in bringing down German 'planes. Whether the higher total was a result of later information or wishful thinking is hard to establish. Much later, official records showed the real number as 90.

in restaurants and thus avoiding the rigours of the war. It was an old story—as long as you could afford to eat out you could carry on as if the war was not happening. The well-off were getting away with not doing their bit and Cassandra was not about to put up with it.

There is a strange irony about the whole of the *Mirror*'s battle with Churchill. Anyone reading the issues for 1940 could not fail to be impressed by the enormous zeal which the paper had for the war effort. It was forever brimming with advice to its readers on avoiding waste, joining the ARP, getting girls to volunteer for productive work and any number of other constructive projects. The tone was one of unbridled enthusiasm and a righteousness which sometimes bordered on the pious. Some unfortunate woman had her dustbin examined by eager reporters who proceeded to castigate her in print because she had not kept her bottles separate from her bus tickets, had not saved her pea pods to use as vegetables and had thrown away a pencil stub which could have been used as fuel! Silly? Well, yes. Subversive? No. And yet subversion was what Churchill was beginning to suspect.

In October 1940 Attlee and Beaverbrook interviewed Esmond Harmsworth (who was Chairman of the Newspaper Proprietors' Association), Lords Camrose and Southwood and told them that the Cabinet had been discussing the irresponsible criticism which had been appearing in the *Mirror* and the *Sunday Pictorial*. It was to stop, or censorship would be introduced which would affect views as well as news. Subsequently Cecil King and Bart were sent to hear Attlee's message in person. A blow-by-blow account of their conversation, and indeed the entire affair, can be found in Hugh Cudlipp's *Publish and be Damned* and Cecil King's published diaries; it is sufficient to record here that Attlee seemed to have no very clear idea of what it was that the government was objecting to. Cassandra was mentioned, as was the 'Live Letters' column, but no specific charges were made. The affair dragged on into the January of 1941 with Churchill writing a string of letters to King which said little more than had been said already. The *Mirror* had been 'rocking the boat' and the fact that it was a popular paper with a sensational style was no defence. However, the row subsided and there was an uneasy sort of truce for a while.

It seems strange in a era when attacking politicians is a national sport and the crucifixion of government ministers is almost compulsory, that in

'Drenched to the skin—his hair dripping with sea water and his life jacket still on his back—this sergeant pilot of one of our fighter planes is brought to a south coast beach.'

those days, the *Mirror*'s comments should have aroused such anger. Churchill, of all people, might have been expected to realise that the paper was, at bottom, on his side. Yet he seems to have got hold of the idea that the apparent support for the war effort was merely camouflage intended to cover fifth column activities. He asserted that it was a well-known trick to pretend to be in support of a policy and then to whittle away at it bit by bit until you eventually manage to destroy the whole thing. His attitude seems to have been little short of paranoid and the reasons for this are hard to fathom. It may well be that, given the enormous strain the man was under, and the fact that Churchill was in a much better position than the *Mirror* to understand just how near we were to defeat, even well-meant criticism could seem an intolerable attack.

In spite of the political battles behind the scenes the war-time paper prospered. Of course, it was much smaller than it had ever been before, a mere 12 pages compared to the 38-page issues of the late thirties. Later in the war it was to shrink to eight pages. Naturally the lack of space meant that the sledgehammer techniques which Bart had pioneered had to be restrained. It was just not possible to use

huge headlines and employ a lavish use of space. Fortunately, part of the Bart ideal was the short, snappy story, based firmly on the belief that nobody reads more than a few hundred words on any subject. So, although the *Mirror* now began to look crowded, it still had a large amount of information in its pages and it was still written in the brief, punchy style which the readers had come to enjoy so much. Space was so short that radio programmes had to be squeezed into the margins between pages.

Another restriction on war-time publishing was the use of censorship and this was particularly onerous on a paper which had made so much use of pictures. Suddenly the pictures were no longer available and, even if they had been, it is more than likely that they would have been censored. Even so, Bart made one notable attempt to improve the situation. By this time he was too old to be considered for the armed forces, and his job as the controlling force on a national paper was too important for him to leave it, but he was determined to see some action. During the Blitz, in the winter of 1940-1, he joined the National Fire Service and managed to get hold of an official vehicle. Together with George Greenwell, a *Mirror* photographer, he covered the worst of the raids, whilst acting as back-up assistance to the local fire units. Even so, he still turned up at the office early each morning to start his normal day's work. Not bad for a man of 56.

The shortage of photographs led to an increased dependence on the cartoon for illustrating the paper. And this was to be a source of considerable trouble. The *Mirror*'s cartoonist was called Philip Zec, young, Jewish, a man with a good reason to hate the Nazis and a great gift for creating the most savage, violent cartoons to appear in the pages of a national paper since the creation of a truly national Press. Zec was a black and white cartoonist in more senses than one; his drawings were great, heavy, terrifying masses of black ink which put forward a simple, straightforward moral. Generally there was precious little chance of misunderstanding a Zec cartoon, it hit you right between the eyes; and if he had any trouble thinking up a really hard-hitting caption he would occasionally ask Cassandra's advice, knowing that he always knew how to hit hardest and in exactly the right spot. Oddly enough it was a bit of ambiguity in a Zec cartoon which nearly got the *Mirror* suppressed.

Early in 1942 Zec had started a series of cartoons attacking the profiteers, the men who sat at home and grew rich whilst other people did the fighting and dying. One of the subjects which came up was the price of petrol and the way in which merchant seamen were being killed off in droves to get the precious juice the country needed. The government had just increased the price by a penny, but Zec wanted to put across the message that petrol cost *lives* as well as money. His cartoon of a half-drowned mariner clinging to a makeshift raft put the point well. His caption was 'Petrol is dearer now' but, on Cassandra's advice he changed this to '"The price of petrol has been increased by one penny"— official'. The sky was about to fall in. Churchill had had enough of the *Mirror*, more than enough, in fact. On all sides he was hearing complaints from people in high office who had been upset by its attacks. He was firmly convinced by now that there was dirty work going on behind the innocent facade. Attempts were made to discover who actually owned the paper. But the subject had become impossibly complicated since the Northcliffe days and no-one could really unravel the whole story of who the stockholders were.

On March 19 Bart and the Editor, Cecil Thomas, were asked to see Herbert Morrison, the Home Secretary and a former contributor to the *Mirror*. Morrison brought out the whole fifth column argument again, but this time reinforcing the previous complaints with an attack on the Zec cartoon which, apparently was supposed to dissuade sailors from putting to sea. Without further ado Morrison intended to suppress the *Mirror*. He went straight to the House of Commons to announce that, under regulation 2D, the paper could be suppressed, but that a preliminary warning had been given.

The reactions of MPs, other newspapers and the public were fairly mixed. There were those among the other newspapers who would not have been sorry to see a successful rival put down. There were MPs, on the other hand, who saw in the threat of suppression a sign of the sort of totalitarian state we were supposed to be fighting against. After a long, rather messy fight in the Commons the matter was dropped.

Even now it is hard to see what all the fuss had been about. There were so many different interpretations put on the offending cartoon that, if it had been intended as a piece of subversion, it was a pretty ineffective one. Possibly the real reason for Churchill's sudden hatred of his old ally was quite a

The battle at sea was also well covered In this shot a spotter 'plane had sighted a U boat and guided two destroyers to it. When depth charges were dropped the U-boat was destroyed.

different one. The *Mirror* had, for a number of years, been moving steadily to the left. It was encouraging Joe Average to express his views; it was encouraging him to be dissatisfied with the status quo. Churchill was by no means a stupid man—could it be that he was already aware of the sort of reaction which the *Mirror*'s political stance was going to provoke in the future? If a popular paper continued to encourage people to criticise the government and everyone else in authority over them, might that not be a terrible force for change in the future?

So, the *Mirror* went back to normal. With one exception: Cassandra joined the forces and for the next five years his readers were deprived of their regular dose of fire and brimstone.

But even the Second World War had its lighter side. As far as *Mirror* readers were concerned that aspect of the war was typified by Jane. Remember the 'Diary of a Bright Young Thing' which had so amused the office girls during the thirties? Well, the war seems to have had an unfortunate effect on the poor girl who developed a most unfortunate tendency to lose her clothes at the slightest provocation. Jane spent most of the war away from her somewhat wet boyfriend Georgie and was engaged on a number of secret missions of national importance. However, the gravity of the situation was not enough to keep her fully clothed, any gust of wind, unexpected sharp object, or foreign villain was sufficient to cause her to strip to her cami-knickers on the spot. Eventually the *Mirror* plucked up the courage to reveal Jane in a state of nature: there was shock, outrage even, but the forces loved it. Jane was responsible for maintaining the morale of our troops, a job which she did superbly well. Even the Yanks were nuts about Jane and she was widely credited with some of the more significant Allied advances. It is reliably reported that even in the Officers' Mess, where most people would not have been caught dead reading the *Mirror*, Jane was considered essential reading and her exploits were followed more closely than those of Rommel. More about Jane and her creator later.

Another bit of fun which the *Mirror* dreamt up was the newspaper for submariners called *Good Morning*. Naturally, by the nature of their work, they spent long periods isolated in uncomfortable and dangerous conditions with the minimum of home comforts. In the normal course of events they would never have seen a newspaper from one voyage to the next. Why not, thought the *Mirror* hierarchy, print a paper which contained all the features, cartoons and light-hearted bits from the *Mirror*. It was a tremendous success; each day the Chief Petty Officer would hand out the new edition

to an enthusiastic readership. Of course, there could be no actual *news* in such a paper, but this was dealt with by including items about the submarine service, the men and their families. So popular was the paper that in 1945 Bart was, at the suggestion of the Admiralty, awarded the OBE. Typically, he neglected to tell people about the honour and even members of his own family only found out about it later on.

However, in spite of the hard work, guts, patriotism and grit which *Mirror* employees displayed during the war, it was not a happy period for journalism. Wars never bring out the best in newspapers, they encourage deception, exaggeration, hatred—and all from the very best of motives. The Germans were once again guilty of every crime under the sun; the Japanese were not only enemies, they were enemies with slanting eyes and yellow skin, and therefore much, much worse. Anyone reading, say, Cassandra talking about slant-eyed sons of Satan could be forgiven for forgetting that these were the same Japanese who had been our noble allies when the *Mirror* first began. This is not to denigrate the journalists, they were merely reflecting the spirit of the times and, when all is said and done, Nazism and Japanese Imperialism were evils which had to be fought. However, to look back on that sort of writing cannot give anybody much pleasure. As the war came to an end the *Mirror* was not only able to rejoice in the victory of the Allies, but to look forward to a new society in which, it was hoped, the old evils would be absent.

A final note of interest—at the end of the First World War the *Mirror* consisted of eight pages and cost 1d. By the end of the Second World War it had eight pages—and still cost 1d! 🌐

Above right *This is the stuff of popular journalism. Kids saved from mortal danger and safely wrapped in warm blankets. A shot like this made better propaganda than all the rantings of poor old Goebbels.*

Right *The crippling of HMS* Kelly *by a German torpedo was the start of a legend and established Lord Louis Mountbatten as a national hero.*

DAILY MIRROR, Monday, September 2, 1940.

Daily Mirror

SEPT 2

No. 11,461 — ONE PENNY
Registered at the G.P.O. as a Newspaper.

CHILDREN'S SHIP TORPEDOED—ALL SAVED

A MERCY SHIP CARRYING 320 BRITISH CHILDREN TO CANADA HAS BEEN TORPEDOED, BUT NOT ONE OF THE CHILDREN WAS HURT.

Singing popular songs, the children landed at a British port last night.

Only casualty was the purser, killed in an accident after the attack.

ACTED LIKE GUARDS ON

Thus Hitler has kept his promise that Germany would not guarantee a safe conduct to ships carrying child evacuees.

The courage of the youth of Britain defeated total warfare. So well had they learned lifeboat drill that their rescue was easily carried out. All landed in Britain yesterday safe and sound.

As they took to the lifeboats the children sang, "O Johnnie, O Johnnie" and "Roll Out the Barrel."

When more than seventy of the children were landed at a British

---

Page 6

THE DAILY MIRROR, DECEMBER 7, 1940

Page 7

DON'T WALK HOLES IN YOUR POCKET

FIT **GOOD/YEAR**
'LIVE' RUBBER HEELS

2 hours' slaying power for 1d

The biggest little meal in Britain 2d

DOCTORS URGE SHELTER DICTATOR

Whose Babe Is Which?

It's You or Munitions

How Kelly Came Home

Their Food Wasted

MAN WITH THE NELSON TOUCH

Torpedo, Bombs, Fog and Storm

BRITISH GRIT IN A BRITISH SHIP BEAT THE LOT

LORD LOUIS MOUNTBATTEN, COUSIN OF THE KING, REFUSED TO ABANDON SHIP, SINK HIS SHIP, H.M.S. KELLY, WHEN SHE WAS CRIPPLED BY A GERMAN TORPEDO OFF THE ENEMY COAST.

Smash America Is Jap Army Demand

ONE BEACH AFTER ANOTHER

"Held Me When I Die"

Enemy "Over the Top"

Right *There was time for a few breaks from the drama of war. This is Jeanne Darcy, 17, making a name for herself with ENSA.*

Left *The Blitz took its toll in East London. Are we downhearted? Well, apparently Mrs Bidecant (right) insisted on inviting homeless neighbours to share a meal in the bombed shell of her own house.*

Right *The young Ralph Lee being taught the ins and outs of a .303— eat your heart out Adolf!*

Breasting the Waves of Fortune

THE SON-OF-A-GUN

With another front now we want all the men we can get ! And hearing this opinion young Ralph Lee thought he'd better learn all he could about rifles. He's having instruction from his father, Driver Lee.

Young Ralph is a member of the same corps (in an honorary capacity), and attends parades every morning.

I ASSURE YOU . . .

More Rail Cuts Coming: BY BILL GREIG

DRASTIC cuts in railway services are under consideration. Ministry of Transport believes there is still

Children's Teeth in War-Time

Even in war time a child's diet *must* contain a proportion of sweet things for nourishment and energy. But sweet things cause acid-mouth which encourages the germs which attack and decay the teeth. To protect the teeth a child's toothpaste should contain plenty of 'Milk of Magnesia,' the most effective neutralizer of mouth acid known. Only in one toothpaste is 'Milk of Magnesia' brand antacid to be found and that is Phillips' Dental Magnesia which contains 75%.

Children who use this pleasant tasting toothpaste regularly, always have the whitest teeth and are practically free from decay with its distressing toothache and disfiguring gaps. Get a tube today.

Sold everywhere, 7½d., 1/1 and 1/10½d.
(Including Purchase Tax).

PHILLIPS' DENTAL MAGNESIA

'Milk of Magnesia' is the trade mark of Phillips' preparation of Magnesia.

Nourishes your
→ **nerves**

ay Travel
Class

at the abolition
London suburban
make more room,
rabazon, Tran-
sted in the House
erday: "In rush
t carry all they
such conditions
gers are allowed
ss carriages with-
t."

Is the Minister
s Cross Station
s the doors of
es are locked?
Brabazon: I hope
e said today will
ation.

Off—

s or

Year

ll have a holiday
mas Day or New
not both.

Labour, Mr. Ernest
he Joint Advisory
nistry last evening
ed production on
d continue without
for Christmas Day

tly contemplates
e no Bank Holiday
t least for workers
war work.

nt was made at
g whether Boxing
ded generally as a
how Mr. Bevin's
arding workers on
will affect those in

d that the alterna-
mas Day or New
war workers does
o Scotland. Some
rs in the north of
o prefer New Year's

t that appropriate
e paid as provided
eements for work-
days.

HARD'S JOB

na of the Nether-
ted Prince Bern-
son officer between
nd Air Force and
British Forces

COVENTRY MOURNS AS 172 ARE LAID IN ONE GRAVE

A city mourns 172 of its people slain by Hun bombs and laid in one grave.

The folk in the picture on the left are those who have lost those 172—children, wives, husbands, sweethearts. They listen to sad and yet brave words spoken by a grey-haired Bishop. He tells them that the Germans can kill their loved ones, but that their spirit no enemy can kill.

The picture above shows those tragic folk moving along the trench which is the last resting place of their loved ones.

And while it represents Coventry's mass tragedy, it reminds too that each one of those hundreds of mourners has an individual sorrow to bear.

See that fireman. A tiny bunch of flowers clasped in his hand, the flowers that he placed in memory on one of those 172 coffins.

We shall remember, too.

ROCKING THE BOAT

Left *It was pictures like these which did so much to strengthen resolve. The tragedy of Coventry made it even clearer to the British people that they were now fighting total war.*

Right *A dramatic heading announces the opening of a new front. Note the sloping headline; if there was an interesting way of grabbing attention the* Mirror *was sure to find it.*

Below *The famous Zec cartoon which almost got the* Mirror *suppressed. Note the written comments by Zec and Cassandra. Bart once told Zec: 'Anything you've got the guts to draw I've got the guts to print.' And he meant it. The final caption was: ''The price of petrol has been increased by one penny.''—Official* (photo courtesy of Lt Col Peter Bartholomew).

He lost his ration book

Above far left *In spite of all its trials the Mirror was not about to lose its sense of humour.*

Above left *The tide begins to turn and German prisoners are seen arriving in Britain. This picture was taken a few days after D-Day.*

Left *A dramatic night shot of a 4½-in rocket-firer in action. Sixty rocket tubes were mounted on a Sherman tank and could be fired separately or in salvoes. The effect was quite remarkable.*

Above *The Allies uncover the horrors of the concentration camps.*

Above right *The news everyone had been waiting for. Hitler's death did not end the war immediately but it brought the end much closer.*

Right *Zec's end-of-the-war warning showed considerable foresight. The caption read, 'Where now?'*

Daily Mirror

MAY 9

Wednesday. May 9, 1945
No. 12,912   ONE PENNY
Registered at G.P.O. as a Newspaper.
+

BRITAIN'S DAY OF REJOICING

In the centre of 50,000

Dense crowds in Whitehall, estimated by the police at 50,000—all cheering like mad—mobbed the Prime Minister when he emerged from Downing-street after his broadcast speech. With the broad grin of victory on his face—and a new cigar clamped between his teeth— Winston Churchill gave his famous V-sign.

Minute past midnight

THE final total surrender documents were signed by the Germans and the three Allies yesterday IN BERLIN. The Channel Isles were to be freed at once.
Hostilities in Europe ended officially at 12.1 a.m. today.

"Here you are—don't lose it again"

Left *Crowds in Whitehall celebrated the victory. Churchill can just be seen in the centre of the shot giving his famous V-sign.* **Above left** *This cartoon, which was famous for its obvious message, was revived by the Labour Party for the 1945 General Election. This was the chap Labour voters were urged to think of when casting their votes.* **Above right** *Not a very dramatic treatment for probably the most important story in world history. Relief that the war was now over prevented most people from realising fully just what this new weapon was to mean.* **Below** *This is the sinking of the British battleship* Barham, *torpedoed in the Mediterranean on November 25 1941. She sank in less than five minutes; 868 men died and 303 were saved. The picture was only published years later when the Allies were well on the way to victory.*

Daily Mirror

WED AUG 15 1945

FORWARD WITH THE PEOPLE

No. 12,995   ONE PENNY
Registered at G.P.O. as a Newspaper.

PEACE

JAPAN SURRENDERS— ALLIES CEASE FIRE

Piccadilly, caught napping, woke up

"Daily Mirror" Reporter

PEACE news caught West End revellers napping — but only for an hour, and then Piccadilly went wild.

At midnight there were not more than a hundred people round Eros. By 1.30 this morning there were thousands—screaming, shouting, dancing and throwing their hats in the air.

When Mr. Attlee announced the Jap surrender there were twelve people outside Buckingham Palace—rearguard of the thousands who thronged the West End for five nights in succession for the great news. One man was shouting for the King.

But at two o'clock the march on the Palace had begun again, and great crowds packed The Mall and Trafalgar Square.

In the area between Marble Arch and Grosvenor Square American troops went delirious with delight.

Jeeps tore down Oxford-street and there was a continual hullabaloo of motor horns, klaxons, bells, police whistles, tin drums, dustbin lids—in fact anything which would make a noise.

A crowd of about 200 American soldiers and sailors with the Stars and Stripes at their head marched down Oxford-street singing "Yankee Doodle Dandy" and "Over There."

And—a gigantic conga line of about a thousand Service men, women and civilians headed by a Scotsman in kilts, marched from Marble Arch, through Grosvenor Square, and continued on their way to Piccadilly.

At 3 a.m. police estimated that the crowds in Piccadilly Circus were as great as those on VE-Day.

For after the Premier's midnight broadcast thousands of people set out from the suburbs in lorries, horse-drawn carts, motor-cycles and cycles (some even walked) in an early morning effort to join in the West End celebrations.

Rockets and fireworks flashed and exploded over the heads of the merry-makers around Eros, and there were cheers for firemen who arrived to tackle a blaze in an office block hit by the rockets.

Sitting on the backs of the

Continued on Back Page

Troops had to rescue the police

TOWNSFOLK all over Britain got up in the middle of the night and lit bonfires. Servicemen fired Verey lights over the country side sailors, soldiers, airmen and Service girls started rafficking in a big way.

And in America, hordes of celebrators—it was only 7 p.m. for them—set out to make a night of revelry that would go down in history.

Civil and military police had to hold back a Liverpool crowd which tried to mob a troopship at Prince's landing stage. Hundreds of bonfires turned the sky into a ruddy glow a few minutes after victory was announced.

Military police were posted to keep a huge crowd out of the White House at Washington. Then troops had to be sent to rescue the military police, who were being crowded against the fences and walls, and take them into the White House grounds.

Eight abroad, Servicemen and civilians marched through Gillingham, Kent, carrying the Union Jack, headed by an impromptu band of dustbin lids snatched from house fronts.

9 p.m. BROADCAST BY THE KING

The King will broadcast at 9 o'clock tonight. There will be a Thanksgiving Service on the B.B.C. at 8.15 p.m.

PETAIN SENTENCED TO DEATH

MARSHAL PETAIN was sentenced to death at 3.30 this morning.

The verdict on the eighty-nine-year-old Marshal was announced after the jury had been conferring for six hours.

When the 20th and last day's session of the trial passed its eighth hour, food was sent in to the jury.

While the jury was deliberating, Madame Petain was informed that she was freed, with no charges against her,

Today and tomorrow V-days "Enjoy yourselves" call by Attlee at midnight

"PEACE HAS ONCE AGAIN COME TO THE WORLD. LET US THANK GOD FOR THIS GREAT DELIVERANCE AND HIS MERCIES." IT WAS THE VOICE OF THE PRIME MINISTER, BROADCASTING FROM NO. 10, DOWNING-STREET AT MIDNIGHT TO TELL BRITAIN THAT JAPAN HAS SURRENDERED.

Japan has accepted the Allied terms without qualification. The Jap Emperor is to order all his forces to lay down their arms and obey all commands of the Allied Forces.

ALLIED ARMED FORCES HAVE ALREADY BEEN ORDERED TO SUSPEND OFFENSIVE OPERATIONS. AN ATTACK BY HUNDREDS OF PLANES WAS CALLED OFF IMMEDIATELY.

In his broadcast Mr. Attlee announced that today and tomorrow will be V-Day holidays.

"Let all who can relax and enjoy themselves in the knowledge of work well done," he said.

Arrangements have been made for the formal signing of the surrender at the earliest moment and President Truman has named General MacArthur as the Allied commander to receive the surrender.

Washington reports last night said that the surrender will probably be signed on a battleship, or on Okinawa, scene of one of the most savage battles of the Pacific war.

Emperor to Broadcast

It was announced in Tokio that the Japanese Emperor, breaking all precedent, would broadcast to the nation at midday (4 a.m. British Summer Time).

In his White House statement last night President Truman said: "The proclamation of VJ-Day must wait upon the formal signing of the surrender terms by Japan.

Soon afterwards, however, came an announcement that President Truman had proclaimed a two-day holiday for all Federal employees on Wednesday and Thursday throughout the United States.

Mr. Attlee went to the microphone in No. 10 to give the news of the surrender after a bewildering day in which the hopes of the world had been raised and dashed again

Continued on Back Page

Forward with the people

The war in Europe was over. A new age was dawning and it would call for new people with new ideas. The *Mirror* was determined to be a major force in shaping that new age. The paper had been moving steadily to the left for years, but now that an election was coming there could be no other place for the *Mirror* but firmly in the Labour Party camp. During the war the paper had championed the common man, the ordinary serviceman, and now those men and women wanted a government which would represent *them*.

The Labour Party approached the *Mirror* for help with its campaign and Bart gave Philip Zec the task of advising them. He went to see Herbert Morrison and was horrified to find that the campaign was not even formulated. Later, in conversation with Bart, Zec was saying that he felt frustrated that the country had been saved by the servicemen, and that they were the people who ought now to have a major say in the running of the country. The government was trying to call a quick election which would be over before many servicemen got home. Wives had written to the *Mirror* saying they would be voting for their husbands. Thus Bart suggested Zec should use the slogan 'Vote for *Them*'. That was the Labour Party slogan and for two weeks Zec worked like a dog designing leaflets and posters to put the message across.

The Labour victory in that election is now a matter of record, but what is not so well known is that Herbert Morrison, who so nearly closed the *Mirror* down during the war, apologised to Zec, saying that he realised that the whole affair of the petrol cartoon had been a mistake. Even that was not quite the end of the affair because, some time later, Zec was walking round the House of Commons with the late Maurice Edelmann MP when they bumped into Churchill. When the introductions had been made the old man said, 'Mr Zec, I believe I owe you an apology. Consider it made.' At last the affair of the cartoon was over.

What sort of paper was the post-war *Mirror*? On May 11 1945, ten days after the death of Hitler, the paper had adopted the slogan 'Forward with the people' which it carried on its masthead. This was to be the key-note of the paper in the new post-war era; it would concentrate on the common man, the working class or lower-middle class average bloke. But what did Joe Average want to read in his daily paper? Support for the Labour Party and concern over important social issues was all very well but for most of the time people demanded a lighter diet. The *Mirror* soon found the subjects which would sell papers: sex, scandal and sensation. It was a heady mixture and it was not long before the paper was in hot water once more.

When John Haigh, the acid bath murderer, was arrested in 1949, the *Mirror* gave the story the full sensational treatment, but on this occasion the paper went just a bit too far. There had been a series of 'vampire' murders in London and, though the *Mirror* never said that Haigh was responsible, the inference was there for anybody who cared to pick it up. Scotland Yard contended that the story prejudiced the chances of a fair trial and, although the *Mirror* modified its account, it still left in details of the vampire crimes. The Editor, Silvester Bolam, was sentenced to three months' imprisonment for contempt of court by Lord Goddard, the Lord Chief Justice. The *Mirror* was fined £10,000.

While Bolam was in jail Bart, Cudlipp and Zec went to see him. According to Zec, Bart was concerned that Bolam should not be demoralised by the experience; he was still the Editor and they were going to bloody well make him feel like the Editor.

The internal politics of the *Mirror* have always involved titanic clashes between the larger-than-life figures who have run the paper. When Bart was finally deposed at the end of 1951 it was, typically, a dramatic episode. It started when Bart phoned Phil Zec and told him that he had received a letter from the board asking for his resignation. Zec, by now a

Two men who had a great influence on the post-war Mirror. **Left** *Cecil Harmsworth King, the cool, detached analyst and* (**right**) *Hugh Cudlipp, the 'whizz-kid' from Wales.*

director of the paper, knew nothing of the matter and told Bart to stay by his 'phone while he discovered what was going on. He then got in touch with Cecil King and invited him to lunch. During the meal it transpired that King, together with a number of other directors, had decided that it was time for Bart to go. He was an old man now and they felt that it was time for a new chairman to take over. Zec had not been consulted because they all knew he was pro-Bart and they had a quorum without him. The key factor in the affair was that Silvester Bolam had voted for Bart's resignation; without his support it could not have happened. Zec was asked to go and see Bart and explain the situation to him. He did—there was a long, painful and highly emotional scene in which Bart, probably for the first time in his life, was reduced to tears. For days he refused to sign the letter of resignation. The one thing which had hurt him above all else was the defection of Bolam. To Bart that was the act of a Judas and he could not forgive it. Eventually he had no choice but to accept the situation and resign. And so one of the most astounding figures in British journalism was, in effect, sacked.

Bart not only made an immense impression on the journalism of this country, he also had a way of dealing with people which ensured that they would

never forget him. Even now, years after his death when many of his colleagues are not so young themselves, anyone who used to work on the *Mirror* can tell you his own Bart story. Ronald Bedford, now the *Mirror*'s Science Editor, had terrible eye trouble when, as a young man, he started work on the paper. He only had one eye and it would only function for reading if he held the paper 2½ inches away from it. One day the Editor, Silvester Bolam, summoned Bedford and told him that Bart wanted to know why he read that way. Bedford explained, also pointing out that he could not help it and if the Chairman didn't like it he knew what he could do. Time passed. Bedford was summoned once more to the Editor's office.

'I passed on your message to the Chairman', said Bolam, 'and he said: "What's the blind fucker doing about it? Tell him to get things put right if he can—and send me the bill".'

In those days medical science was not equal to the task of putting Ronald Bedford's eye in order (though it has done so since), but Bart's offer showed him and everyone else that the tough, hard-boiled old martinet had another side to him.

What of the men who followed Bart? The next Chairman was Cecil King and a more different character it would be hard to find. Whereas Bart was short, King is very tall, Bart was all fire and intuition, King is cool, analytical and detached; Bart had little formal education and was contemptuous of intellectuals, King is the son of a Professor of Oriental Languages, went to Winchester and finished his education at Christ Church, Oxford, where he took a history degree. King once summed up his own character in a conversation with Zec.

'*You*,' said King, 'are a thinking man. *I* am a critical man. I may not be able to build a wall, but if you build one and there is a single brick out of place, I will notice.' It was this facility for criticism which, as far as the *Mirror* was concerned, was to cause his downfall. During the period of the Wilson Government in the late sixties, King wrote an article entitled 'Enough is Enough'. It was a serious attack not only on the Labour administration but also on Wilson himself. For the *Mirror*, now solidly behind the Labour Government, enough was too much and Cecil King had to go.

The third, and undoubtedly the best-known, of the *Mirror* Chairmen in the post-war years is Hugh Cudlipp (now Lord Cudlipp). He had left school at 14 and became a reporter on the *Penarth News*. By the age of 24 he was Editor of the *Sunday Pictorial* and it was this which earned him the title of whizz-kid which, strangely, still seems to fit him perfectly, even though he is now in his late sixties, a knight and a peer of the realm. Cudlipp has been described as 'impulsive, self-assured and bold; cynical (but soft-hearted too); ingenious and energetic; fiercely controversial' and many other things besides. As far as the public is concerned Cudlipp must be the only *Mirror* Chairman who is a well-known public figure. Bart was so fearful of publicity that, even when his wife had persuaded him to live in a suite at the Dorchester, he would go in by the tradesmen's entrance, and when he was offered a peerage he turned it down flat. King was always known as a shy man. Cudlipp, on the other hand, is a familiar face; usually seen with a large cigar in his mouth, not infrequently with a glass in his hand, he has learnt to ride the waves of publicity with the consummate skill of a champion surfer. And there is one other reason that the public is familiar with Hugh Cudlipp for, almost alone among top journalists, he has written lucidly and entertainingly about the life of Fleet Street and, in particular, the *Mirror*.

One of the more curious aspects of the post-war papers is the odd, and almost entirely one-sided, relationship which the *Mirror* struck up with the Russians. Whereas the rest of the Press confined itself to more-or-less sorrowful editorialising on Russian behaviour, the *Mirror* decided on frontal attack. The first example of this is the front page

which Cassandra wrote when the head of the Soviet secret police was to visit Britain with Bulganin and Krushchev in 1956. Ivan Alexandrovich Serov was described as 'an odious thug', 'the Himmler of the Soviet Union', 'this grisly creature', 'this revolting butcher' and 'this murderous turnkey'. The front page was headed, 'Who wants this odious thug in Britain?' Exactly how Serov felt about Cassandra is not recorded. However, 1956 was the year of the Suez Crisis and the Soviet suppression of the Hungarian Revolution, so we must assume that Ivan Alexandrovich ended his year a happy odious thug.

Nothing daunted, the *Mirror* had another crack on May 17 1960. Nikita Krushchev had just lost his temper at the Paris peace conference because of his pretended outrage at the capture of an American U2 spy plane over Soviet territory. The *Mirror* addressed an entire front page to him and set it in a type size which made it look more like a poster than a newspaper. 'MR. K! (If you will pardon an olde English phrase) DON'T BE SO BLOODY RUDE! PS Who do you think you are? STALIN?' The use of the word 'bloody' caused a bit of a stir

The Cold War was well under way in 1956 but there was nothing cold in Cassandra's welcome to Serov.

The Mirror *campaigned vigorously against armed intervention in Egypt. It used the front and back pages together to make a greater impact and dubbed itself the paper with two front pages.*

and that particular front page has become quite famous. However, there is a quote from Krushchev himself which has largely been forgotten and deserves a revival. The old tyrant commented, 'As God is my witness, my hands are clean and my soul is pure!'

Not all the *Mirror*'s messages to Russian leaders were so belligerent. In February 1967 there was a front page headline in Russian which welcomed Kosygin to London with the words, 'Welcome to Britain, Comrade Kosygin!'

Whether the Russians ever took any notice of this sort of rhetoric is not important. The *Mirror*'s success lay in the fact that it knew what its readers would like to say if they were given the chance and it expressed the public view loud and clear. After all

the diplomatic nonsense of 'condemning in the strongest possible terms' the odd 'bloody' came as a refreshing change.

Having just mentioned Suez, this is a good point at which to examine the *Mirror*'s treatment of that sorry affair. In 1956 President Nasser of Egypt announced that he was going to nationalise the Suez Canal. This step would effectively block a vital route and was intended to put pressure on the Western Powers to cease support for Israel. Eventually Britain, France and Israel launched attacks on Egypt but were forced to withdraw by pressure of outside opinion, especially from America where there was considerable interest in hastening the decline of Britain as a world power.

At home there were serious divisions over the Suez issue. The Left, including the Labour Party, felt that the era of gun-boat diplomacy was over and that it was reprehensible to resort to war in order to settle the issue, especially when the result could be a third World War. The *Mirror* agreed with this view and printed the views of many eminent people who felt the same way. Among those quoted were Hugh Gaitskell, the then leader of the Labour Party, and the Archbishop of Canterbury. In order to give these views sufficient prominence the paper turned its first sheet sideways and printed it as a broadsheet so that both the front and back pages were covered. The heading was 'ARE THEY ALL LIARS AND SCAREMONGERS?'

Eventually the crisis was over and the danger of a full-scale war which would have included Egypt's patron Soviet Russia, receded. The *Mirror* was proud to have championed the cause of peace and diplomacy as an alternative to war, though subsequent developments in the Middle East show that conflict was not to be so easily avoided and the danger of a major war starting in the area is still as real as ever.

One of the most noteworthy features of the *Mirror* during the sixties and early seventies was its series of 'shock issues' which dealt with a wide variety of subjects from pollution to road safety, child abuse, and so on. Each report was given the sledghammer treatment; a front page with one enormous picture and a headline which was legible from several yards away. Pollution was symbolised by a girl in a gas mask with the headline 'England's Green and Poisoned Land'; road safety was emphasised by a huge picture of a skeleton driving a car and the slogan 'Keep Santa Claus safe this week!' If the *Mirror* of previous decades had been sensational it was merely tame compared to the treatment that these stories got. Each issue was one which directly concerned the reader and about which he could do something, if only he would. The paper was determined to stir its readers in a way they had never been stirred before.

Certainly the shock issues had their effect and people were disturbed enough by the facts to write to the paper in their thousands. The public reaction was just what the *Mirror* wanted; it sold papers and it had valuable social consequences. However, there was a problem. Being shocking in this way is a bit like using four-letter words; do it occasionally and you will get noticed, do it frequently and you will be ignored. Eventually shock, horror and sensation had outlived their usefulness and the *Mirror* subsided to a quieter tone. Not that it ever completely abandoned the shocking approach, but it reserved it for occasions when there was something to be shocked about. Even then there were problems. After World War 2, after Auschwitz, after terrorism, assassination, mass murder in Vietnam, genocide in Cambodia, who the hell can you shock? Even the prospect of the long-awaited nuclear holocaust no longer produces the same reaction as it did back in the fifties and sixties. Whatever moral and philosophical conclusions can be drawn from this are quite outside the province of this book. But when a newspaper has made a living from sensation and there are fewer and fewer sensations left, where does it go next? There is at present no answer to this question, though I strongly suspect that both Tony Miles, the Chairman and Editorial Director, and Mike Molloy, the Editor, are thinking very hard to find one. Perhaps in the sombre and perilous '80s the readers will look to the paper to reflect, as it did in the '40s, their aspirations, their interests and, above all, their concern.

Two events during the sixties were of great importance. The first was in 1961 when new offices were opened in Holborn Circus. The huge office block, which is still the paper's home, was necessary because business was booming and there was a great need for room in which to expand. With typical gusto the *Mirror* made a story out of the move and entitled it 'THE HOUSE THAT 14,000,000 READERS BUILT'.

The other major event came three years later when, on June 9 1964, the *Mirror* was able to announce that its circulation had reached 5,018,000, a truly remarkable figure. It had clearly outstripped all its rivals including its closest competitor, the *Daily Express*. For a considerable time the *Mirror* was able to boast the highest circulation in Europe, then the world and, finally and with tongue in cheek, the Universe. Eventually that boom passed and now the paper has a less dramatic circulation, though a figure of 3¾ million is

not to be dismissed lightly even today.

One subject which crops up in the *Mirror* with particular regularity is that of the Royal Family. In past ages, as we have seen, royalty were treated with the respect due to lofty beings who scarcely seemed even human. When the *Mirror* managed to scoop the picture of Edward VII lying dead there were murmurs about the impropriety of publishing such a photograph. When the paper commented on the abdication crisis there were more mutterings about sensationalism and the necessity of the Press preserving a dignified silence. But the *Mirror* knew only too well that the appetite of the British public for details about its Royal Family is insatiable and sells newspapers as few other topics can.

However, it was the Princess Margaret affair which caused greatest disapproval. The Princess wanted to marry Group Captain Peter Townsend but was being dissuaded from doing so because he was a divorced (gasp!) man. She hesitated for a considerable time and the *Mirror* was prompted to say publicly what most people had been saying privately for ages. A headline proclaimed 'Come on Margaret! Please make up your mind'. In case

Do you get the impression that Krushchev and the Mirror *were not the best of friends?*

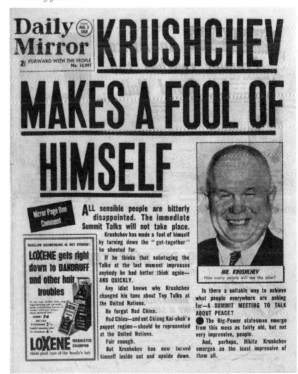

Daily Mirror
MON NOV 4 1957
2½   FORWARD WITH THE PEOPLE
No. 16,763

CAN THE SPACE DOG RETURN FROM THE NEW 'RED MOON'?

SPACE No. 4 **MIRROR**
NOV. 4, SPACE YEAR ONE
—and see Pages Six and Seven

RUSSIA SCORED ANOTHER DRAMATIC SCIENTIFIC TRIUMPH YESTERDAY WHEN SHE FIRED A NEW SPACE SATELLITE NEARLY 1,000 MILES ABOVE THE EARTH WITH A DOG INSIDE IT.

A Russian scientist was reported as saying that the dog would be brought back to earth alive. But British scientists said they thought it most unlikely that the dog would survive.

Details of the new " Red Moon," announced by Moscow Radio early yesterday, revealed that—

Its **SHAPE** is like a bullet—not round like the first satellite launched a month ago.

Its **SPEED** is 18,000 m.p.h—about the same as satellite No. 1.

Its **WEIGHT** is 1,120lb.—half a ton. The first satellite weighed only 186lb.

Professor Bernard Lovell, in charge of the world's biggest radio telescope at Jodrell Bank, Cheshire, said yesterday:

" It is a very dramatic and spectacular demonstration of Russian achievement in science and technology."

Mr. Kenneth Gatland, vice-chairman of the British Interplanetary Society, said: " It's simply fantastic."

The dog in the new satellite is a

■ Continued on Page 24

Russians astonish the world again

★

BRITISH SCIENTISTS SAY:

'DRAMATIC' 'FANTASTIC' 'SPECTACULAR'

● It is a Husky like this which is 1,000 miles above the earth in Sputnik II. This picture was taken by an automatic camera in a Russian rocket fired last month. The dog returned to earth safely.

It is a grim thought that the new " Red Moon " might say " Woof, woof ! " as well as " Bleep, bleep."

anyone had missed the point a poll was held so that readers could vote on whether she should defy the forces of the Establishment or conform to tradition. Hugh Cudlipp said afterwards that the headline was meant to be a cheerful comment from a voice in the crowd. Certainly there must have been many people who felt as he did. But to say so in a newspaper was widely condemned, mainly by the newspapers which hadn't thought of the idea first.

Of course, the storm passed and, for many years we were all treated to the usual run of royal weddings, births, polo matches, state occasions and holidays at Balmoral. All faithfully recorded by *Mirror* cameramen. But then another storm broke. For some time the satirical magazine *Private Eye* had been entertaining its readers with details of Princess Margaret's friendship with Roddy Llewellyn, a man many years younger than herself. The story had not had a wide circulation; the Princess usually appears in *Private Eye* under the name of Yvonne (the Queen being Brenda). The national Press had preserved a tactful silence but, eventually, the suspense was too great and it became quite obvious that Princess Margaret was going to get divorced from her husband Lord Snowdon. Naturally it was a scandal which kept the papers in front page material for a very long time. But strangely much of the blame for the furore fell on the shoulders of the *Mirror*'s columnist Paul Callan. This was largely because of a two-part article called 'The Brothers' which was published in March 1978 and which went into the lives of the Princess, Roddy Llewellyn and his brother Dai, in intimate detail. Callan's writing is witty, sharp, occasionally cruel—and always very readable. His sensational revelations came in for a lot of criticism—much of it hypocritical—but they also fascinated the readers. Paul Callan tells us that he feels his chances of a mention in the Honours List are a trifle dimmed.

One of the developments which has worried newspapers in the post-war period has been the growth in popularity of television. If people can turn a knob and get immediate news and entertainment, why should they buy a newspaper? In the old days they were thrilled to see newspaper pictures of, say, the siege of Port Arthur, even if they got them a long time after the event. Now they expect pictures from the far side of the world to be flashed on their screens via communications satellites. As I write the Iranian Embassy siege is still fresh in the memory. How can a newspaper be expected to compete with TV coverage of events as they happen?

However, the *Mirror* had, in a sense, been through all this before. The cinema had broken the monopoly of photo-journalism and had badly affected *Mirror* sales in the 1920s. That was an experience which the paper was not anxious to repeat. It was avoided very neatly; instead of competing directly with TV, why not join it? As a result of this the *Mirror* has become a great adjunct to TV watching. If you want to know what your favourite star likes for breakfast, why he gave up taxidermy to become an actor or what sign of the zodiac he was born under, the *Mirror* will almost certainly enlighten you. And this sort of coverage has been extended to film stars and pop musicians as well. By embracing show business whole-heartedly the *Mirror* has protected itself from the possible harmful effects which mass communication could have had.

This leads to another very characteristic feature of *Mirror* journalism. We noted that even in the early days the paper had a knack of mixing serious news with trivia. This knack has subsequently been developed into an art form. The technique is really quite simple; you place a piece of light reading right next to a piece of serious news, often giving equal prominence to both. Just glancing at a couple of recent issues I can see Jim Callaghan losing control of the Labour Party right next to Prince Edward watching his brother fall off a polo pony, and a rather nasty blackmail case shares the front page with a trailer for a series of extracts from a book about sex in America. This manner of presenting the news leads to charges that the *Mirror* thus trivialises important events and makes no attempt to distinguish them from the nonsense of daily life. The invasion of Afghanistan becomes only as important as 'Who killed JR?'. But this does the paper a disservice; the *Mirror* knows only too well that its readers are not avidly interested in politics or economics and have only a fairly vague notion about the importance of world events. If they were presented with acres of serious comment (as Rothermere tried to do back in the twenties) they not only wouldn't read it, they would all quickly change allegiance to *The Sun*. Thus the heavy stuff is sandwiched between the light; if you want the jam you must eat some bread with it. This may sound rather patronising (and, I should stress, it is not, as far as I know, an official editorial policy, it is my own interpretation of the paper's attitude) but why should the news not be presented in an attractive fashion? Not everyone has the stamina or the interest in current affairs required by *Times* readers.

Left *The space race was in its early stages in the fifties. But in Britain, typically, most people were more worried about whether the dog could be brought back. The* Mirror *was quick to pick up this point and ask the question which was on everybody's mind.*

There is another aspect of this popularising of the news. Do you remember all those leading articles before World War 1 which argued the pros and cons of Calvinism, etc? And have you read a *Mirror* leader recently? A bit of a difference, eh? There is no longer any room for casual philosophical speculation, the *Mirror* now gives straight, concise opinions on important political issues. It is not a paper renowned for the subtlety of its views; whereas *The Guardian* can never reach any conclusion without lengthy debates of the 'on the other hand . . .' variety, the *Mirror* reviews the argument in a few punchy phrases and comes out with an answer, frequently in one sentence and usually in bold type, just in case anyone was about to miss the point. Of course, this sort of discussion is easy to dismiss as simplistic. On the other hand (Oh God! now I'm doing it) newspapers are largely in the business of confirming their readers' prejudices. Very few socialists read the *Telegraph* just to hear the other chap's point of view and it seems unlikely that there is a great rush of Conservatives all eager to see if *The Morning Star* has any right on its side.

In recent years the *Mirror* has faced really serious competition for the first time. Of course, in the past, there has been rivalry with the *Daily Express* but this was to some extent a phoney war since the two papers appealed to quite different readers. However, when the ailing paper *The Sun* was taken over by Australian Rupert Murdoch and turned into a sensational tabloid, a rivalry was born which was to hurt the *Mirror* quite seriously. At present the papers have circulations which are roughly equal (around the $3\frac{3}{4}$ million mark) and, for the first time in many years, the *Mirror* can no longer claim to have Britain's highest daily sale.

Although the competition is in deadly earnest as far as the rival publications are concerned, for the public there is a touch of farce about the situation which enlivens it considerably. For one of *The Sun*'s most popular features has been its nude pin-ups on Page 3. So popular have these pictures become that the phrase 'Page 3' has actually worked its way into the language. For a while the *Mirror* copied the idea and carried pictures of tits and bums on page 5 or 7. But then the idea was suddenly dropped. The Editor, Mike Molloy, told an inquisitive reporter from *The Times* that he had done it, 'to see whether there was something more interesting to go in the paper.' He also told *The Times'* London Diary correspondent that:

'A rumour has been circulating that this is part of a policy to go upmarket, but no decision has been taken. Newspapers change imperceptibly, and we just decided to drop the nude for a while. She can always reappear if the demand is there.'

Apparently the decision was not greeted with any great emotion by the readers but, shortly after, the paper introduced its 'Next-to-Nothing Girls' whose function was to do more teasing than stripping. 🌐

Daily Mirror

Sixty-eight thousand tons of concrete ... five thousand tons of steel ... thirty-five thousand square feet of glass ... The sky's the limit!

Daily Mirror

Yes, it was an exciting day! The Daily Mirror, Britain's most popular newspaper, opened its new home in Holborn Circus, London, E.C.1

THE HOUSE THAT 14,000,000 READERS BUILT

The Mirror makes a new landmark in London

Above *The* Mirror *eventually outgrew its traditional home and was moved into the tower block overlooking Holborn circus where it still lives.* **Below left to right** *Princess Margaret has provided the Press with stories about her love life for years. The attention she was given by the* Mirror *was not always welcome and was the cause of some criticism.*

Daily Mirror

EUROPE'S BIGGEST DAILY SALE

MARGARET AND TONY DIVORCE

By AUDREY WHITING

MARGARET AND TONY Going their two ways.

DAILY Mirror

BRITAIN'S BIGGEST DAILY SALE

COME ON MARGARET (AGAIN!)

COME ON MARGARET!

Please make up your mind!

David Holmes in police quiz

Daily Mirror

Six PARTY days to Christmas ! ! ! ! ! !
So the Mirror appeals
to the women of Britain . . . . . .

2½d. Monday, December 19, 1960 ✦ No. 17,732

KEEP SANTA CLAUS SAFE THIS WEEK !

- Christmas is nearly here. Only six party days to go.

- Office parties. Works parties. Private binges in the pubs. So have fun. Have a drink.

- But, remember, if you drink AND drive this could be your last Christmas. Or some other nice bloke's last Christmas—and YOUR fault.

- One hundred and fifty-five people died on the roads over the holiday period last year. It was the blackest Christmas on record—and party drinks were blamed for most of the slaughter.

- So to every wife, mother and sweetheart the Mirror today urges: See that the man in your life is there to carve the turkey on Sunday.

- Help to make it a WHITE Christmas on the roads. See that your favourite Santa Claus takes care.

- The Daily Mirror, Britain's most popular daily newspaper, does not like losing its readers.

Left Road safety at Christmas and the paper was determined to ram the message home.

Above More shocks. People often objected to reading this kind of thing over breakfast, but they kept on buying the paper just the same. The shock tactics may have been crude but they were nothing if not effective.

Right One of the most famous shock issues. Cruelty to children has seldom been exposed so effectively.

Daily Mirror

How Britain saw it—on television

3d, Saturday, April 15, 1961 ★ No. 17,830

YURI'S DAY OF GLORY

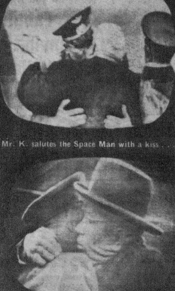

The Space Man salutes Mr. K

Mr. K. salutes the Space Man with a kiss . . .

. . and follows it up with another . . .

while the Space Man's wife and mother look proudly on.

In their thousands, the people of Moscow march to honour their hero.

A GLITTERING Kremlin reception the most splendid since the lavish days of the Czars, set the seal last night on a day of glory for Major Yuri Gagarin, the first man to conquer Space.

Top Soviet leaders, headed by Premier Krushchev, hugged and kissed the twenty-seven-year-old hero as 2,500 guests—including the whole of the Diplomatic Corps—cheered.

It was the climax to a fantastic day . . .

A day that began with a tremendous and moving welcome at Moscow Airport—the drama of which was shared by millions of people in Britain who watched a sensational first-ever TV link-up between Britain and Russia.

And the viewers in Britain saw some of the most moving and excitingly dramatic pictures ever shown on television screens.

There was the tense moment of anticipation as Russian TV cameras picked up the Ilyushin turbo-jet airliner and its fighter escort.

CANDID

There was a revealing "candid camera" shot of Gagarin's wife, slim and bespectacled, and his father and mother, typical Russian peasants, and o t h e r members of his family, waiting—almost bewildered by the grandeur of the occasion—for the big moment.

The camera caught one brief moment of nervousness.

Apart from that G a g a r i n carried himself with dignity and poise.

In fact, he played his part to perfection.

Then came the moments of drama and emotion.

DRAMA as he saluted, and delivered his personal report to Mr. K—a report carried direct to the crowd and viewers by microphone.

EMOTION as Gagarin, his report completed, was kissed in father-like embrace by Mr. K and other Soviet chiefs.

DRAMA as the official congratulations and embraces over, Mr. K finally put an arm round the Spaceman and led him to the spot where his wife and parents were waiting.

EMOTION as he embraced and kissed his wife and family.

Reception like 'days of Czars'

There were more memorable shots from Red Square later.
● Gagarin's h e a d - s c a r f e d mother, seeming almost on the verge of tears for the ovation to her son.
● His wife, wearing glasses, smiling a trifle self-consciously when Krushchev praised her as a "woman of great strength" and one who had not tried to dissuade Gagarin from his Space flight, but supported him.
● Gagarin making his own special salute to the crowd—a double arm wave almost like a mock "surrender" signal, and then a boxer's clenched hands of victory.

Apart from some interference during the Red Square telecast, reception was extremely good over the 1,500-mile link from Moscow—first to Tallin in Estonia, then to Helsinki, to Stockholm, Copenhagen, Brussels and finally to the B B C Eurovision "switchpoint" at Tolsfield Hill, Kent.

LAST WORD from Major Gagarin as he left the Kremlin reception: "I would rather undertake another flight into Space than go through those celebrations again.

"The girls go ga-ga over Gagarin"—P3.

CHRISTINE IN COURT

—as 'Lucky' Gordon is accused

By BARRY STANLEY

RED-HAIRED Christine Keeler, alleged to have been attacked by club-singer Aloysius (" Lucky ") Gordon, denied yesterday that earlier this year she was expecting a baby by him.

'Was I having a baby by this man? No, I was not..'

CHRISTINE KEELER ... pictured during a visit to the Film Festival at Cannes, on the French Riviera.

America to build a super plane

THE FRIEND Paula Marshall, pictured in London yesterday. Miss Keeler is said to have been attacked at Miss Marshall's Flat.

Left *Major Yuri Gagarin, the first man to conquer space. In spite of the Cold War he became a hero outside his own country—schoolgirls used to send to Russia for autographed photos.* **Above** *The Profumo affair was regarded as the scandal of the century. It rumbled on for months as reputations were ruined and lives were wrecked.* **Below left** *Poor old Mr K gets another wallop from his favourite daily. I wonder if he told his newsagent to cancel his order?* **Below right** *The Mirror displays a rash of cyrillics as Comrade Kosygin arrives in Britain. Much of his popularity stemmed from the fact that people called him Cosy Gin!*

Daily Mirror

MR. K!

(*If you will pardon an olde English phrase*)

DON'T BE SO BLOODY RUDE!

PS

Who do you
think you are?
STALIN ?

Daily Mirror

ДОБРО ПОЖАЛОВАТЬ В ВЕЛИКОБРИТАНИЮ, ТОВАРИЩ КОСЫГИН

[Welcome to Britain, Comrade Kosygin !]

THE DAILY MIRROR puts out the flags today for a most important visitor at a most important moment in world affairs.

Alexei Nikolaevich Kosygin, Prime Minister of the Soviet Union, who books in at Claridge's, London, today, is one of the two most powerful men on earth.

ALEXEI NIKOLAEVICH KOSYGIN — Chairman of the USSR Council of Ministers, Order of Lenin (twice), Order of the Red Banner, Hero of Socialist Labour.

HOPEFUL

Continued on Page Two

Far left *The Mirror reached a record circulation unmatched by any other paper. Its influence at this time was enormous and its voice was heard throughout the country.*

Left *The assassination of Martin Luther King shocked millions. His fight for racial equality had won him widespread admiration.*

Below left *The Vietnam war was the first to receive full Press coverage. For the first time the public got to see the horrors of war with a minimum of censorship. It was a war with many victims and no heroes.*

Right *Britain takes its first steps into the EEC. In spite of the enthusiastic headline it was to be a decision which is still controversial a decade later.*

Below *Dead fish in a polluted river became a symbol of the poisoning of our industrial society. This sort of image was the Mirror's forte—not a picture easily forgotten.*

DAILY Mirror

BRITAIN'S BIGGEST DAILY SALE

- **Dateline: Westminster, Oct. 28**
- **Time: 22·16 hours**
- **The historic decision is made**

'YES' TO EUROPE!!

MAJORITY: 112

AFTER THE COMMONS DECISION, MR HEATH SAID:

Now we stand ready to take our first step into a new world full of new opportunities | Our historic decision has been made: the British people accept the challenge

FULL STORY
—BACK PAGE
HOW YOUR
MP VOTED
—PAGE TWO

MIRROR COMMENT

SHOCK ISSUE

Oh yes. It's a special issue of the Daily Mirror today.

This "shock issue" is dedicated to blasting us all out of our complacency over the massive problem of POLLUTION.

The British Way of Life (and death)

WHAT is the Government doing about it now?
WHAT is the Government planning to do about it in the future?

IN TOMORROW'S MIRROR—
PETER WALKER, SECRETARY OF STATE FOR THE ENVIRONMENT, TALKS TO MIRROR READERS

The Killing Waters

TROUBLED WATERS: last month thousands of fish died in the River Derwent at Borrowash, Derbyshire. The river board unsuccessfully tried to find out the reason. Cause of the fishes' death: unknown.

TURN TO PAGE 7

Daily Mirror

EUROPE'S BIGGEST DAILY SALE

3p · Friday, March 9, 1973 · No. 21,507

One dead and 214 injured in blasts

OUTRAGE

- **The bloody blitz that hit London**
  —Page Two
- **Ten held in big swoop at airport**
  —Page Three
- **The horror and the devastation**
  —Page Seven
- **Lunchtime blast rocks a Ministry**
  —Centre Pages

A man representing the law comes under attack. This is Caesar James Crespi, 21 years a barrister, injured in the Old Bailey bomb outrage yesterday.

Left and above *The troubles in Northern Ireland have occupied much space in the British Press for many years and will probably do so for a long time to come. The slaughter in Londonderry and the bombing in London left much of Britain confused—the English have always found it impossible to understand the affairs of their Irish neighbours.*

Above right *A British soldier makes his own comment on the situation in Northern Ireland.*

Right *We're in! But will we stay in?*

Death of a Nation

Above far left and left *1974 was the year that Britain first realised just how bad a state the economy was in. Following a winter of strikes, the three-day week and power shortages many people believed that we were heading for financial doom. Perhaps we still are.*

Far left *Marje Proops launches an attack on sexual ignorance. She was appalled by the lack of sexual knowledge among the general public and, being a forceful lady, spelt out the facts very clearly for the uninitiated.*

Left *Only the* Mirror *could arrange for the Loch Ness monster to make an appearance at the Queen's Silver Jubilee celebrations.*

Above and right *John Pilger and photographer Eric Piper revealed to the world the genocide in Cambodia. Nothing like this had happened since World War 2 and it was largely because of this report that massive public donations were sent to try and help the stricken nation.*

MONEY TO BURN: Children play with useless banknotes. Some families use them for lighting their cooking fires.

" This one machine replaces six Linotype operators. "

SHE'S FIRST IN THE FIELD

SHARON FIELD went into modelling straight from school and now, at eighteen, she's in a class of her own.

Sharon is such good form that she has been signed up by one of London's top agencies.

And to make sure she stays in the running, Sharon, from Rainham, Essex, keeps fit by jogging.

Picture: KENT GAVIN

Far left *The* Mirror *has never been far from the action but in 1978 a murder took place on its doorstep. The bandits got away with £200,000 and killed a security guard.*

Left *Guess who? Uncle Harry turns out on closer inspection to be HRH the Prince of Wales. His sense of humour has always been popular with the public and accounts for his frequent appearances in the* Mirror*'s pages.*

Below far left *In the mid-seventies the* Mirror *introduced computer technology into its production process. This wry comment contained a grain of truth.*

Below left *This sort of picture was an attempt to compete with* The Sun*'s page 3. Later, Editor Mike Molloy was to discontinue the practice to see whether he could not find something more interesting to put in. Well, you can try Mike, you can try . . .*

Right *Trust the* Mirror *to find the only redeeming aspect of the Iranian Embassy siege. Her name was Nooshin Hashemian—not as tough as the SAS but much, much prettier.*

Below *The* Mirror *may contain a lot of fun and pretty girls but it never forgets its political mission. The unflattering images of Maggie Thatcher were part of a campaign to attack the policies of a government with which the paper disagreed very deeply.*

Andy Capp meets Marje Proops

Any selection of the cartoons and features which have made the *Mirror* so popular must, of necessity, be a personal choice. The following are our favourites, if we have missed one of yours—sorry!

For all those who remember the Second World War the *Daily Mirror* is inseparable from Jane. If Vera Lynn was the forces' sweetheart, then Jane was their bit of crumpet. Bernard Levin once wrote that, 'Jane, when I was a schoolboy, was the last word in naughtiness, the 1940s equivalent of the 1970s unexpurgated editions of de Sade'. Not that Jane was ever kinky, indeed she was prim to a remarkable degree. Of course, her clothes did keep coming off, but never for *that* reason. She was just a pretty, decent English girl with a steady boyfriend and a remarkable facility for getting hooked on bits of barbed wire, or walls, trees, the ropes of barrage balloons. Anything, even a very slight breeze, would remove Jane's clothes. For much of the time these natural disasters would merely strip her down to her bra and cami knickers; however, there were occasions which were eagerly awaited by her thousands of fans when she was stripped to the buff. Even so, there was always a well-placed obstacle which prevented the gentle reader from getting too excited. Levin also recalls that she frequently had invisible nipples and that her breasts varied in size—sacrilege indeed! Insult the politicians all you like, Sir, but leave that lady alone!

Jane was to be found in the *Mirror* from 1932 to 1959. As we have said earlier, her real notoriety did not start until the war when she was made responsible for maintaining the morale of the Allied forces. When the cartoon eventually finished the public, and even the other newspapers, went into

mourning. Jane's adventures were later reprinted in a book, and there was even an attempt to revive her by starting a 'Daughter of Jane' series. But it was all too late. The sort of tantalising naughtiness on which she relied for her appeal vanished with the Swinging Sixties.

Her creator was W. Norman Pett, a rather severe and sober looking man who reminds one more of a school-teacher than a creator of naughty cartoons. He lived in a cottage in the Cotswolds and sent his work to London by train. Every few weeks he would travel to the *Mirror* himself and have a conference

Right *Christobel Leighton-Porter who was Norman Pett's model for the Jane cartoons. This photograph was recently discovered in a second-hand bookshop and shows why Jane was such a great favourite with the Allied forces* (photo via John Hall).

The career of Jane spanned nearly three decades and she didn't age one day. Here are some of her more famous moments. Her successor, Patti, never really caught on in the same way.

with his scenario writer, John Freeman. They would plan 18 strips at a time and Freeman was chiefly responsible for concocting all those fascinating situations in which Jane could lose her clothes. It was once calculated that, in a ten month period, Jane dressed, undressed or was forcibly deprived of her clothes 51 times.

She was widely credited for having helped the war effort. The RAF noticed that, on days when Jane stripped completely, their missions were more successful. The result was that, against all the dictates of good security, the *Mirror* received 'phone calls saying, 'There's a big show on next Monday, for Christ's sake make sure she gets 'em down!' *Round Up*, an American forces' paper in the Far East said: 'Well, sirs, you can go home right now.

Jane has given her all. The British 36th Division immediately gained six miles and the British attacked in the Arakan.' It is also said that her picture adorned the first tank ashore on D-Day. However, when her adventures started to be syndicated in American papers the stories had to be toned down so as not to offend their more delicate sensibilities.

Those who believe that Jane was merely the work of Norman Pett's over-active imagination are quite wrong. She was drawn from life using as a model pretty Christobel Leighton-Porter. Christobel still gets asked to make appearances as Jane.

After the war it was our heroine who took part of the blame for the Labour Party's victory in the General Election of 1945. It was suggested by certain Tories that many people who were not politically committed had read the *Mirror* in order to see Jane and had been influenced by the paper's Labour propaganda.

Eventually even Jane had to be retired. Although

she was not a day older than when her career had started 26 years before, in 1959 she and Georgie got married and disappeared, quite literally, into the sunset.

Another strip girl, called Patti, was launched but things were never the same again.

If you were a newspaper Editor and someone approached you with a great idea for a strip cartoon about a drunken, idle, dishonest good-for-nothing who never takes his hat off (even when he's beating his wife), the odds are that you would politely show him the door. But Reg Smythe, creator of Andy Capp, had just that idea and it has proved to be one of the greatest cartoon hits ever. Andy has been going strong since 1957 and his adventures are now translated into a multitude of languages. Although everything about Andy Capp is strictly rooted in the North of England (in fact, he was originally commissioned for the northern edition) he has an appeal everywhere he goes. Even southerners, whom he despises for their habit of drinking weak beer, love him. In fact, so popular is he that the short-lived *Mirror Magazine* published his biography. By a strange coincidence Andy was born in the same town where his creator now lives—Hartlepool, Co Durham. That was on July 10 1917. Andy did have a childhood of sorts: his first recorded words were 'Get knotted', he smoked in his pram and, before he could walk, he had learnt to waddle with the aid of a billiard cue. However, he very quickly attained middle age, pausing only briefly on the way to marry the long-suffering Florrie who was unfortunate enough to trip over him while he lay in a drunken stupor outside his local. Ever since, Andy

has, in the usual manner of cartoon-land, stayed the same age—fiftyish. He is a passionate sports fan, an even more passionate drinker, he never pays debts and he has a relationship with his wife which even Marje Proops couldn't sort out. Fortunately, since Florrie can give as good as she gets, there is no immediate prospect of a divorce. But just in case things ever turned really nasty and Andy had to flee the country he has a string of foreign aliases. In Austria he is Charlie Kappl, in Denmark Kasket Karl, the Finns call him Latsa, the Germans Willi Wacker, the Dutch Jan Met De Pet, and so on in 1,000 newspapers in a multitude of countries including Thailand, Borneo and Red China. How long can he carry on like this, people ask? Well, when Reg Smythe was telephoned to ask if he would draw a special cartoon for this book he agreed instantly (thanks, Reg!) and wanted to know what sort of cartoon we would like. We left it to him . . . there was a two-second pause and then: 'Right, well I think I've got an idea now, how about this . . .'. Reg keeps on drawing Andy Capp day in day out and all he asks from the *Mirror*, apart from money, of course, is that they don't make him leave Hartlepool and come to London more than once a month—like Andy, Reg is not very fond of London.

However, it was not international acclaim which told Reg he was famous. His mother, who lives in the North East, had been reading and cutting out the cartoon every morning since it first appeared. She was always proud of Reg but never realised how he had 'got on' until he showed her a photograph. It had been taken at a Cartoonists' Awards Dinner and he was chatting with half a dozen other blokes, all in evening dress. She stared at it for a while with a reverence generally reserved for the insurance

Reg Smythe, the creator of Andy Capp.

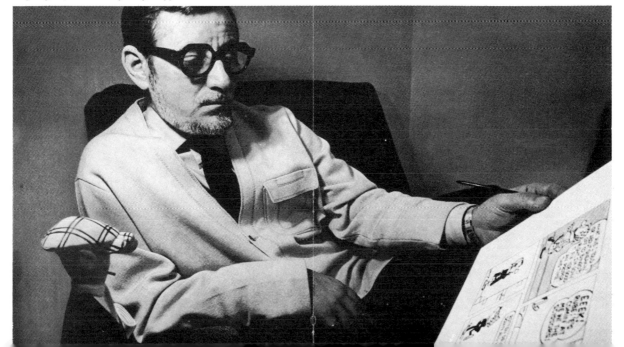

The lad himself. Not content with being in trouble with Florrie, the rent man and the bookie, Andy got into a row with the legal profession of Brazil. This cartoon, which appeared in Jornal da Tarde, *was claimed to insult lawyers!*

man and Prince Philip and said: 'Eee, our Reg, you look just like one o' *THEM*.' Reg had arrived.

When cartoon strips first appeared in the *Mirror* they were very firmly based on American prototypes. However, it had been decided that they should have an English image and therefore we were presented with anglicised versions of some famous American characters. The most successful of these was Garth, first published in 1943 and drawn by Steven Dowling. Originally he was based on heroes such as Superman but he took on a life of his own and has become the paper's longest running strip. Quite what his appeal is I can't say. The adventures move so slowly that sometimes they seem to have ground to a halt. Our muscle-bound hero lumbers from one peril to the next and the dialogue is limited to gems such as; 'The Anglais is getting away!' Since that may be the only text in a whole episode things tend to drag a little. Nevertheless, Garth may not appeal to us but he has a considerable following and looks set to complete many more adventures.

Most prominent among *Mirror* cartoonists must be Philip Zec, who not only drew all the cartoons during the Second World War, but also went on to become a director of the paper. Mr Zec is one of the few people left who remembers the great days of Bart and the Tabloid Revolution. He was kind enough to agree to be interviewed for this book and we were very pleased to be able to include his reminiscences. He is a tall man, Jewish of Russian extraction, who refers to himself as 'a good Cockney'. He has an endless store of anecdotes about the *Mirror*, Fleet Street and the famous people of the not-too-distant past; but mainly his stories reveal a deep respect and affection for two men, Bart and Cassandra.

Zec was introduced to the *Mirror* by Cassandra. Bart had decided that what he really needed during

the war was a first-rate political cartoonist who could be relied upon for the important task of boosting morale both among the public and the armed forces. Since the *Mirror* was already very much the forces' paper it was doubly important that they employ the right man for this job. Cassandra knew Zec from his days in advertising and when he was given the job of finding the best war cartoonist available it was to his old friend that he went for advice. Zec was at this time running his own studio and was just about to join the RAF. Cassandra told him that the only idea they had come up with so far was a well-known cartoonist, called Louis Raemakers, who had been very popular during the First World War. Could they get him? But Zec knew that, in the first place, the man was now in his 80s and, secondly, he had already been approached by another paper. Bart was not pleased; he wanted a cartoonist. And when Bart wanted something Bart damn well got it—or else. Cassandra came back to Zec and suggested he try his hand at the job. But Zec was no cartoonist and never had been, also his war-time plans were already made and it was a bit late to change them. Even so, under the Old Pals Act, Cassandra managed to persuade him to draw six cartoons which were immediately shown to Bart. The old man was impressed; he wanted Zec to be his cartoonist and to draw one cartoon a day for the duration. Starting *now*.

Zec arrived at the *Mirror* in some bewilderment and, not knowing quite where to go he stopped a passer-by in a corridor and asked which office he should go to. The stranger, a shortish, rotund, bespectacled chap with white hair, conducted him to an office, pointed to a desk and said, 'You sit here', and then left. Shortly after, a well-spoken and rather elegantly dressed man appeared and wanted to know, not unreasonably, why Zec was sitting at his desk. The man was a Mr Lambe who used to write a gossip column called 'Lambe's Tales'. When

BUCK RYAN

BEELZEBUB JONES

POPEYE

GARTH

This page and overleaf *Some popular names from the* Mirror*'s cartoon history. The strips were largely based on American models but many of them took on a distinctively English air. Garth is the longest-running strip and his adventures have become a trifle more risque in the eighties than they were originally. Why the big ox always gets the girl I'll never understand!*

GARTH by Martin Asbury, John Allard and Jim Edgar

THE PERISHERS by Dennis Collins and Maurice Dodd

THE FOSDYKE SAGA by Bill Tidy

THE MR MEN by Roger Hargreaves

he was told about the mysterious stranger who had acted as Zec's guide the light dawned; that description only fitted one person—Bart. He went to see him and came back an hour later grinning. Yes, Zec was quite right, he was to sit there. Bart had decided that there was no place for a gossip columnist during war-time and had promptly given Mr Lambe the boot. However, Zec was not to feel badly about it, Mr Lambe had a cheque in his pocket which adequately explained his cheerful grin.

The story of Zec's war-time activities has been told earlier in this book. But the affair of the petrol cartoon was by no means the end of his strange experiences at the *Mirror*. At one point in the war a group of RAF blokes wrote in to the paper asking if perhaps someone could send them an unwanted piano. Cassandra publicised their plea and suddenly the entire building was swamped with pianos, harmoniums, guitars and other assorted musical instruments. It was war, and if our airmen needed a musical instrument then they were certainly going to get one. The result of all this was that one day Cassandra started to play a harmonium which was hanging around unused. Zec began to accompany him on the guitar. Neither was a expert musician but they could both manage a bit of a tune. Zec remembers, for the record, that it was 'Sweet Adeline'. The door opened and some stranger stuck his head into the room. 'What do you think you're doing?' he asked.

'Well,' said Zec, 'He's playing the harmonium and I'm playing this guitar.' The head was removed.

'I admire that,' said Cassandra.

'What?'

'The way you just stood up to the Financial Director.'

'How the hell was I supposed to know who he was?!'

Time went by. The door re-opened and Bart appeared.

'What are you two up to?'

'Well, he's playing the harmonium and I'm on the guitar, but what we *really* want is a drummer.'

'Oh well,' said Bart, 'I can play the drums a bit . . .'

Zec, as has been said, eventually became a director of the paper. Though before that he was in charge of all the cartoons in the *Mirror* and was the man responsible for introducing Andy Capp to ever-grateful readers.

Cassandra has already appeared in this story before, and it is right that he should do so again for he was more than a talented columnist, he was also one of the great legends of Fleet Street and is still remembered now, 13 years after his death. His real name was Bill Connor and his writing career began with composing advertising copy. This was not the sort of job which gave his creative talents sufficient scope and it was therefore fortunate that he met Bart. His version of the meeting went like this:

''Can you write a column?'' asked Bart. Like the man who was suddenly asked whether he could play the violin, I replied: ''I don't know. I've never tried.'' He said ''Start now''—and sure enough I've been sawing the catgut ever since.'

Cassandra's style was usually grumpy and his irritation with politicians, bureaucrats, doctors (whom he hated) and other undesirables would sometimes burst into fury. But he was rarely uncontrolled; he knew exactly how ordinary people felt about those who ruled their lives and he reflected their feelings precisely. Naturally he had many memorable battles with all manner of people. His part in the arguments with Churchill is probably best remembered. Cecil King wrote, by way of excuse, that Cassandra was 'a hard hitting journalist with a vitriolic style'. Churchill replied sourly that, 'throwing vitriol is thought to be one of the worst of crimes'. After the famous affair of the Zec cartoon (in which Cassandra was involved), he joined the army, remarking as he went: 'Mr Morrison can have my pen—but not my conscience, Mr Morrison can have my silence—but not my self respect'. He returned to his column after the war with the immortal quip: 'As I was saying when I was interrupted, it is a powerful hard thing to please all the people all the time.'

Cassandra could be ferociously brilliant; on one occasion he tracked down Senator McCarthy, the leader of the infamous witch-hunt for American communists, and bearded him at his dentist's surgery. Cassandra asked the unlucky Senator a few penetrating questions about his indefensible policies then informed him that he had no wish to shake hands with him and, furthermore he had no desire for the signed copy of McCarthy's book which he had just been offered. The witch-hunter paled for a moment and then said, 'Jeez, that's straight shooting!' However, Cassandra could also be very wrong. On one famous occasion he wrote scathingly about Liberace, the pianist. It was an article which did Cassandra no credit at all, a crude attack on someone who, by his flamboyance, had offended the more sober-minded. Liberace could not ignore the article. In the short-back-and-sides 1950s, public reputations could be damaged by such publicity. He sued for libel, and won, and the *Mirror* was stuck with a bill for £8,000 in damages.

But it would be unfair to finish talking about Cassandra with an account of one of his mistakes. His considerable talent was recognised in 1966

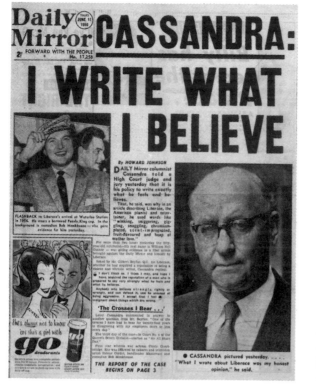

Many people read the Mirror *just to see what Cassandra was saying. When he attacked Liberace there was a law suit which cost the Mirror £8,000. And that was in the days when you could take the wife out for a meal, have a taxi home, and* still *have change out of £8,000!*

when he was given a knighthood. Although he was not a man with much time for the shabby farce which we call 'public life' he was duly touched by the honour. A year later his health failed and he died on April 6 1967. Few journalists have been so widely mourned as was Sir William Connor. The tributes came in profusion, often from the very people he had so vigorously attacked. Few people were able to resist his honest, grumpy, but compassionate style.

Of the *Mirror*'s political cartoonists one of the best remembered is Vicky. Born in Berlin of Hungarian parents his real name was Victor Weisz. His father died when he was only 14 and Vicky supported his mother by drawing caricatures of famous personalities such as Fritz Lang, Max Schmeling, Marlene Dietrich and Conrad Veidt. His ability got him a job on the paper *12 Uhr Blatt*. When Hitler came to power Vicky, a known socialist, was an obvious target for the Gestapo. It was only his

Hungarian nationality which saved him from a concentration camp. His friends sent him to England in 1935 and he became a British citizen in 1946. He worked for the *Mirror* from 1953-8 and was noted for his vicious satire and the savage lampoons of public figures. Readers often complained that his pictures of starving children made them sick at the breakfast table: 'It does them good', was the short reply. The politicians, on the other hand, with a perversity for which they are well known, sought his original cartoons avidly and would often phone the *Mirror* in order to ask for the cartoon in which they had been so thoroughly pilloried.

In an interview with Milton Shulman, in *Picture Post*, Vicky was complaining that some politicians were harder to draw than others. Some had absolutely no recognisable features. Among the offenders was the President of the Board of Trade. The year was 1951, the man was Harold Wilson. Who knows, perhaps that's why he took up the pipe and the Gannex?

Although Cassandra is dead, the *Mirror* is not without modern talent. In 1970 the well-known journalist and writer Keith Waterhouse started to write a regular column. Waterhouse has chalked up an impressive list of journalistic awards and his fictional character Billy Liar has become a household name. When he is writing his column, however, he knows only too well how to dip his pen in the vitriol. On the day that the government decided to increase gas charges and dog licence fees by an enormous amount Waterhouse started his column:

'The cost of gassing yourself because you cannot afford to pay £4 for a dog licence will be going up by 29 per cent this year.' Ouch! Cassandra may be dead but his ghost must be laughing.

Another Mirrorman who has become justly celebrated is the reporter John Pilger. He is, at the moment of writing, Journalist of the Year and his work on the Vietnam War and the genocide in Cambodia has won him considerable popular acclaim. What is particularly significant about his story 'Death of a Nation' is that the *Mirror*, which normally sticks closely to Bart's dictum that nobody ever reads more than a few hundred words on any subject, spread the article over eight pages. An unprecedented step and a brave one. Generally the British public has little idea about far-flung places. You could offer a fiver to anyone who could point to Cambodia on a map and not lose your money. However, on this occasion the *Mirror*, and Pilger, decided that, like it or not, the public was going to learn about the worst outrage since Hitler's murder of the Jews. Definitely one up to the *Mirror*.

Marje Proops, surely one of the paper's most famous faces, a family friend and the foremost of the 'agony aunts', sits in an office infested with houseplants which she refers to collectively as 'The Jungle'. On her office wall is a small cartoon of a housewife chained by the neck, writing a letter. She begins, 'Dear Marje . . .' Marjorie Proops started life as Rebecca Marjorie Rayle, daughter of a Jewish family living in Stamford Hill. She became a freelance fashion artist and was eventually noticed by Hugh Cudlipp, then Features Editor of the *Mirror*, who offered her six guineas a week to work for the paper. However, in 1939 a fashion artist was the lowest form of journalistic life. She later married Sydney Proops and had a son, Robert.

Eventually Marjorie left the *Mirror* to go and work for Hugh Cudlipp's brother Percy at the *Daily Herald*. The now-defunct *Herald* was a Labour paper of even redder complexion than the *Mirror* but Marje has always referred to herself as a 'sentimental socialist' meaning, presumably, that she is more interested in the things which affect the lives of real people than in 'issues'. The advice columnist of the *Herald* died suddenly and Marje took over. It took a lot of study before she felt qualified to do the job, but she managed to enlist the

Marje Proops, Britain's top agony aunt, dispenses advice, sympathy and the occasional kick in the behind.

help of Eustace Chesser, a psychologist, who gave her a lot of help. Eventually Hugh Cudlipp invited her to the *Woman's Mirror* to start the 'Dear Marje' column for which she has become famous. The *Woman's Mirror* was eventually taken over by *Woman*, but 'Dear Marje' ended up in the *Daily Mirror*.

Advice columns have changed tremendously over the years that she has been involved with them. People used to ask if they should wear gloves to a cocktail party, or whether long engagements were a good idea, or was it possible to fall in love twice? Now the questions tend to be of the 'How many orgasms should I have?' variety. Marje's reputation for giving plain, straightforward advice has earned her a wide following among all the *Mirror's* readers, men as well as women. But she has other talents as well and has risen in the company to the post of Assistant Editor, a far cry from her days as a fashion artist.

If you observe *Mirror* readers on a bus or tube you will be surprised just how many of them start their paper at the back and read forwards. This strange habit stems from the great readability of the sports pages and is due in large measure to the efforts of two men, Peter Wilson and Frank McGhee.

Wilson started at the *Mirror* at the same time as Hugh Cudlipp and was one of the early band of pioneers who turned a stodgy paper into a popular and successful one. During the course of his career, which spanned 40 years, he picked up the tag of 'The Man They Can't Gag'. This was an idea which Hugh Cudlipp dreamed up when Wilson was having a spot of trouble with boxing promoters who disliked the things he was writing about them. Of course, nobody ever seriously tried to gag him but the fearless assertion that he was ungagable lent him an aura of daring which brought some extra drama into the reporting of sport.

Many famous Fleet Street journalists have been involved in one of the *Mirror*'s most popular features —the Live Letters column. To name but a few— Hugh Cudlipp, Bill Connor (yes, *that* Bill Connor), Bill Herbert, Cyril James, Robert Balmforth, Edwin Radford and Leslie Gilbert.

The column was the brainchild of Hugh Cudlipp who, in April 1936, was the Features Editor of the paper. Talking to Richard Jennings, the leader writer, Cudlipp said: 'The letters columns in the national papers today are "dead letters". What we need in *The Daily Mirror* is a "Live Letters" column'. Thus was born 'Live Letter Box' on April 20 1936. The man entrusted with the first letter was the late Cyril James, a freelance journalist. He was paid 2/6d for editing the letter and writing a witty reply to it. He was promised 2/6d for every other letter that appeared. But, as the initial response was so great—200-300 letters—the financial arrangement came to a rapid conclusion!

Cudlipp's idea took root and the 'Live Letter Box' developed into a national institution—'The most widely-read daily newspaper column in the world'. And 44 years later 'The Old Codgers' Live Letters' column is still as popular as ever with an average weekly post of 800-900 letters. A few years ago it celebrated its three millionth letter. Typically, it was from two readers living in a basement flat in Brighton, Sussex who offered follow-up information about the night attire of Eskimos! 'Do Eskimos wear pyjamas?' a reader had wondered. The readers in Brighton were able to solve the problem as they had lived in the icy wastes of North America. Their Eskimo names were A-Shela-Piuyiuyuk (The fine one) and Kookatuk (The tall one).

The Old Codgers leave no stone unturned in attempting to solve the most esoteric problems posed by readers!

They also run a highly successful 'Live Letters Landladies' service—at no charge—which thousands of readers take advantage of every year, and a 'Good Grub Guide' which is followed by many people on holiday.

The annual Christmas Appeal raises thousands of pounds for worthy causes. Why? Because the readers are generous by nature and love to help those who are less fortunate than themselves.

In short, the Old Codgers are friends of the family to the millions of *Mirror* readers.

What then is the final word on the *Daily Mirror*? There isn't one. The paper is three-quarters of a century young and is still developing. Marje Proops told us that, above all, the *Mirror* is a 'virile' paper which will continue to grow and satisfy the needs of its readers for many years to come.

Below and below right *Phil Zec, though he had never drawn a cartoon before, became the loudest voice of the* Mirror *during the war. His hatred and contempt for Nazism was powerful stuff. Often he had to draw a cartoon in only three hours, and sometimes even quicker.* **Right** *Vicky, as he saw himself, and one of his cartoons. This satirical look at Harold MacMillan and Duncan Sandys was typical of his abrasive style.*

The hour of reckoning

"I would emphasise that the next few days will be marked by extra-ordinarily powerful U·S·A attacks to achieve a breathtaking decision." (Nazi Radio)

Breathtaking!

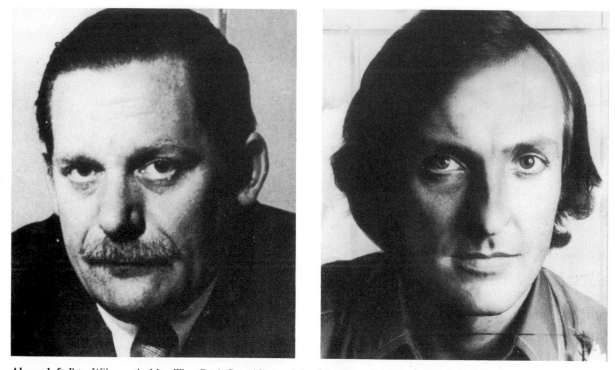

Above left *Peter Wilson—the Man They Can't Gag.* Above right *John Pilger. Last year he was Journalist of the Year, a title he richly deserved and had won not for the first time. The men who run the* Mirror *today:* (below left) *Tony Miles, Chairman and Editorial Director, and* (below right) *Mike Molloy, Editor.*

DAILY Mirror

Tuesday, November 11, 1980   12p   • • •

FOOT FIRST!

MPs pick the man who will take on the Tories

MICHAEL FOOT swept to victory last night in the battle for the Labour leadership.

Although the result was expected to be desperately close, Mr. Foot defeated the favourite, Denis Healey, by 139 votes to 129.

Now he is Labour leader as as long as he wants.

If Right-winger Mr. Healey had won, there would have been a long drawn-out dispute over the leadership.

For Labour is committed to a new system of electing the leader after a special party conference in January.

But Mr. Foot will enter any new contest as the undisputed choice of the Parliamentary party, the favourite son of the trade unions and the red hope of the predominantly Left-wing constituency parties.

His election continues Labour's Leftwards surge which has dominated all recent party conferences.

Mr. Foot is farther Left than any post-war Labour leader. At 67, he is also the oldest.

The party will now attempt to present a united front against the

By TERENCE LANCASTER
Political Editor

Tories. It could be difficult.

But defeated Mr. Healey made a brave start by declaring immediately after the result: "I shall run for deputy leader — as I am sure Michael would have done if I had won."

Mr. Foot's double-figure majority was an enormous psychological blow to the Right.

It is obvious that he must have attracted many Centre MPs and even a smattering from the Right itself.

The Tories were as jubilant as Labour's Left. They feel that Mr. Foot will be an easier man to fight at the next election than Mr. Healey.

WINNER: Michael Foot with his wife Jill after the victory.   Picture: MIKE MALONEY

and Thatcher tells the nation
NO GOING BACK

TOUGH: Thatcher last night

By JOHN DESBOROUGH

THERE will be no let-up in the Tories' tough economic policies, Premier Margaret Thatcher warned last night.

She said the Government would not betray the people by seeking popularity now and sacrificing all hope of future stability and prosperity.

This means that there will be no reflation of the economy to give temporary relief.

Mrs. Thatcher, who was

speaking at the Lord Mayor's Banquet in London's Guildhall insisted that six per cent was all that could be afforded for public sector pay rises.

It was more than many workers in the private sector would get.

Some would get nothing at all, and people on short-time had taken a real fall in pay.

Mrs. Thatcher added: "I am not declaring war on the

unions or their leaders. But I am challenging their illusion that government can be a universal provider."

If the public sector unions took more, it would mean less for those in private industry.

She said that after two years when real earnings had gone up sharply "we now have no alternative but to accept a reduction in the country's standard of living if investment and employment are to recover."

Mrs. Thatcher said the

● Turn to Page Two

MIRROR COMMENT: LABOUR'S CHOSEN LEADER PAGES 2 and 3